Hidden Women of the Gospels

Hidden Women of the Gospels

KATHY COFFEY

ORBIS BOOKS

Maryknoll, New York 10545

Third Printing, April 2004

Library of Congress Cataloging-in-Publication Data

Coffey, Kathy.
    Hidden women of the Gospels / Kathy Coffey.
      p. cm.
    Originally published: New York : Crossroad Pub., 1996.
    Includes bibliographical references.
    ISBN 1-57075-477-2 (pbk.)
      1. Women in the Bible. 2. Bible. N.T. Gospels.—Biography. I. Title.

BS2445.C64 2003
226'.0922'082—dc21

2002023985

For my daughters,

Colleen and Katie:

in these pages,

find Christ's welcome

to all women.

Contents

Foreword

More than anything else, I found in these pages the "power to draw forth." Kathy Coffey has coaxed these hidden women to life, urged their beauty, courage, pain, and struggle to be named. She has given back to each one a life and, in doing so, beckons us toward deeper transformation.

I felt this power in a most incredible way as I read through the stories. I couldn't stop reading. It was as though in every woman I found kinship. In every hidden woman I met a part of myself. Perhaps most amazing of all, as I read these stories and pondered their implications for my life today, I found my memory in a whirl. Suddenly I was recalling the hidden women of my own ancestry. There they were, women of whose lives I know so very little, only a few stories to help me give them a face and historical form.

These ancestors were also hidden women—rural women of America, who worked hard, gave birth to many children, offered kindness and kinship, "stood by their men," and received little or no applause from the world for all their effort. At least they had a name and at least they have not been forgotten completely. The bits and pieces I know about them continue to inspire me.

There is the story of my paternal great-grandmother. I have heard about such things as her love of flowers, her kind ways, her tireless efforts to help others amidst her own frugal life. The picture of her that I love the best is the one my father's first cousin described: "I can see Aunt Katie walking down those mud roads, an umbrella in one hand to protect herself from the heat and a bunch of flowers clutched in the other, on her way to help her daughter with the eleven children."

Then there's the picture of my grandmother Anne who found herself pregnant in her forty-seventh year, binding herself so tightly that no one, not even the adult children, knew she was pregnant until after a healthy daughter was born. Amazing story, that one.

I can also hear in my mind the utterly painful description my mother gives of how, four days after her high school graduation, her own mother died of hemorraghing while giving birth to her thirteenth child, who also died. My mother, the eldest daughter, bore much of the responsibility of raising those children, even after she married. It was no easy life for those hidden, rural women. I admire them greatly. Their lives inspire me and often bring me to tears when I think of the heavy burdens which their hearts and bodies bore.

The power that Kathy Coffey's book has to draw forth these stories from my memory still amazes me. Why did they come to my mind? Why now? I think that, somehow, these women of my ancestry wanted me to know that they too were women of the Gospel—not of the time of the historical Christ but in the time of the Christ who lives forever.

If I look around, as Kathy Coffey did, I see that these hidden women continue to be everywhere in my life. I know it is time that I stopped looking past or through them, or over their shoulders, ignoring them, these many hidden women of my own era. I long to go to them, weep with them in their sorrows, laugh with them in their brief brushes with happiness, affirm them for their goodness and their resiliency, lift their children in the air with joy, and stand in solidarity with them in their just angers. Yes, fight with them and for them:

for employment and equitable benefits, for justice in the courts when they are raped and abused, for freedom when they are trapped in the muckholes of poverty, addiction, and degradation. Kathy Coffey has called to me to look more closely at my modern world, as well as to look more deeply into those well-kept secrets tucked between the words and pages of the Gospels. I know that if I keep returning there, seeking the unseen women, that I will find a radical transformation of my life waiting for me.

JOYCE RUPP

Introduction

"The Bible is a library," intone the scripture professors solemnly. While this metaphor helps to understand the different kinds of literature in the Bible, it may intimidate those for whom "library" connotes hushed and stuffy spaces.

What if, instead, we thought of the Bible as a house full of characters? What if from every nook and hearth, every crevice, corner, kitchen, bay window and balcony, turret and garden tumbled forth women, with stories to enchant and entertain? What if, furthermore, the women had been silent for centuries, and burst out with a pent-up energy that strutted, spun forgotten tales, cavorted, swirled, clicked castanets, and pirouetted? What if, finally, they had so much in common with readers today that they could weave a fabric of similarities, a whole tissue of parallels to our dilemmas, our joys, our failures and frustrations?

Enough of "what if?" Let's open the doors and windows, invite the hidden women forward. Intrigued, we tease them out because they have much to tell us. Not only do they charm us; they also give us another perspective on our tradition and a new ownership of it.

Such an entry point is vital for women trying to reclaim and own a tradition that has been dominated by men.

When most of the characters in a Bible story are male, women have a hard time identifying—or fitting a word in edgewise! In the past they have solved this dilemma through a variety of mental contortions. Miriam Therese Winter describes these gymnastics: "If the shoe doesn't fit, wear it anyway and walk funny."

But her work and that of many others has begun to shift the terms and adjust the fit. For years, women have worn an ill-fitting, scratchy, uncomfortable garment—wrong-side-out. Now we are learning to reverse that clothing, tailor it to our size, mold it closer to our contours. We're delighted to discover the comfort and fit that result. For some people, male language and images of spirituality have gradually lost their usefulness, and for others they have become a straightjacket. Women are finding that men are not the only religious authorities, that in fact we have an inner authority, the Spirit within. As a woman interviewed in *The Feminine Face of God* said, "I have spent a lifetime acquiring expertise in a spiritual language that is not my native tongue, and now something in me is violently protesting, 'No more. No more.'"[1]

As we turn from a foreign language and become more fluent in our "native tongue," we may face the same charge that was hurled at Jesus: "On whose authority do you do these things?" His reply could also be ours: "On the authority of God in me." That Spirit empowers us to use an ancient Midrash technique of Jewish scriptural study to imagine the women who were with Jesus throughout his life. When John said that if all the things Jesus did were recorded, the world itself could not contain all the books, he might have meant the stories of these women.

Of the 1,426 people given names in the Hebrew scriptures, only 111 of them are female. The proportion is twice as great in the New Testament, but there, in contrast to Andrew, James, John, and Judas, we meet the Samaritan woman, the Canaanite woman, the widow of Naim. That

nomenclature seems as odd to women today as would refer-
ences to the Woman of Tucson, the Milwaukee Lady, or the
Wife of Jack. For that reason, the hidden women of the
Gospels have been given names. Their stories, which have
hovered in the white spaces between the lines, here take on
color and flesh.

Over time, women may have been edited out of the
Gospels, but they were originally present at every juncture
of Jesus' life, from his conception through his resurrection.
This book follows that chronological sequence, imagining
the women whose encounters with Jesus affected them profoundly. Engaging him led to a wide gamut of new directions
and challenges, failures, healings, hopes, disappointments,
exaltation, confusion, tragedy, joy springing from disaster,
service, and serenity. So too, Jesus learned from women,
looked to them for support, and drew strength from their
friendship. In whatever ways they touched each other, they
bore the indelible marks of the meeting afterward.

This work of the imagination is one of the necessary
directions Carolyn Osiek identified in her ground-breaking
book *Beyond Anger*. She writes:

> Because feminine images recur elusively but persis-
> tently in our religious tradition ... they tell [us] that
> the symbolic feminine has been valued and cherished
> in at least some phases of our history, even if concrete
> historical women have not. They give eloquent wit-
> ness to the contributions and essential role of femi-
> nine presence in a Church in which the masculine is
> the consciously operating norm.[2]

Jesus' friendships and even brief contacts with women
broke the taboos of a patriarchal society and encourage us to
continue as freed, redeemed, and resurrected people today.
Women find God not only in officially sanctioned places, but
also in their lived experience. Jesus modeled that discovery

by drawing on the everyday for his theology: he didn't talk much about dogma and ritual, but turned instead to vines and lakes, bread and birds, lamps and sheep for his images.

Most chapters of this book contain parallels between the hidden women of the Gospels and readers today: the questions raised by their experience, the similarities to contemporary life. The chapters conclude with questions for reflection or discussion, inviting individuals or groups to choose those that "ring a bell." These can then become tools for uncovering the holiness in their own lives. This crucial process is encouraged in the belief that revelation didn't stop when the last Evangelist set down the pen. God continues to disclose God's self to us: wherever we live, whoever we are, whatever we do.

Elizabeth Johnson proposes in *She Who Is* that women have a block to imaging themselves as Christ which men do not have.[3] If the gender gap prevents our developing that image most central to the Christian life, then it is time to broaden our images and narrow the gap. *The Women's Bible Commentary* counsels us to seize "occasions to confront androcentrism, to explore precisely how women have read themselves into the texts, and to recognize the urgent need for women's own parables, women's own narratives."[4]

We know the satisfaction that comes when the eye doctor tests various lenses, then finally clicks in the right one. "That's it!" we crow, surprised by the sudden clarity. This book is a shift in the lens, a step in a new direction.

ANNUNCIATION

Artists clutter the picture
with lilies, cherubim,
a book. They should show
the void: immense and gaping,
an abyss yawning, ignorant
aimless, hollow, unredeemed.

Intense as laser in her
such seeding, such turmoil
surging to birth
it made the lilies look
limp, the cherubs bony
the book blank.

She saw the tension: a
world pivoting on its hunger
poised for her answer
balanced against a child,
a brittle sword.
Then she said yes.

I

Susanna,

the Shepherd Woman

(LUKE 2: 8-20)

To tell you the truth, I'd had it with sheep. The stench of the animals clung to my hair, pervaded every scrap I owned. Their incessant bleating drowned any thought in my head. No matter how often I washed, I couldn't get the oil of lambs off my hands. I went to sleep exhausted and woke up tired. Shepherds are the rejects pushed to the outskirts of town, and something sinister in me whispered that the townspeople were right. Why would clean people risk a smelly, rowdy crowd contaminating their children? Wherever we went, people pulled out buckets and mops to mask our odor. We lived so close to beasts, maybe we'd become subhuman ourselves.

Worse than that suspicion was my husband's betrayal. Of course I was young and naive when I married Mark, but it surprised me how easily he fell in with his buddies, how uproariously he laughed with them, how soon he forgot me. He was a hard worker and this was our first real job, so I guess I should have admired his dedication. Once I had watched his sinewy arms corraling the sheep, his back bent over the flock that was our livelihood. But arms and backs don't talk. Was this drudgery the peak, the fun-filled youth my grandmother remembered so nostalgically?

One night changed everything. I slept in my usual stupor when Mark jabbed me rudely in the side. His voice shook with terror; he pointed upward. The skies above our fields were silvery, filled with music and wings. I would remember it afterward, whenever I watched the quick pivot of birds or the soft flutter of a moth at the lamp. Then came a voice that contained all music, soothing our fears, promising us good news.

"Don't you know who we are?" I wanted to interrupt. "If you've got a message for all people, you don't give it to the scum of the earth!" But there was no stopping this song. It must have echoed back to the beginning of the world; it resonated far into the future. "Glory to God in the highest heaven and peace to God's people on earth."

Ever afterward, when I have seen a tightly curled bud or the newest spring green, I have remembered that honeyed cascade, that night bursting with stars. There was a sheen on it as though all new life were contained there. One night could not hold so much loveliness; it has spilled into every day since then.

Not that I've discovered perfect bliss. I still get crabby, and Mark has grown more crochety in old age. But I often think: whatever else happens, I have had this. I was there that night. I could die happy because I would still cherish that scene in my mind, hear that music in my heart.

And to think we almost missed it! Some of the men wanted to crawl back into bed; some of the women were too frightened to come. But a lion-like force in me roared: "Let's go to Bethlehem! Now!" I couldn't wait for them to quibble; I ran youthful, free, blood pumping and every sense alert.

Racing with feet pounding and side aching, I wondered. Had we missed the news? Forsaken and alone, had we not heard a message everyone else knew? How puzzling, that the

Messiah would be lying in a manger. I'd often filled a rude trough for our flock; but I'd never put a baby there. Wouldn't the Savior be born in a palace, soothed by sweeping peacock fans? Funny, I never questioned how we'd get past the armed guard that would surround the Messiah.

When we arrived, the young couple looked just as puzzled as we did. I saw the mother's quick, instinctive gesture, reaching to protect the child. We must have startled her—or she got a sudden whiff of sheep!

The men did most of the boasting, but I couldn't blame them. It's not often that a shepherd gets to flaunt his authority or tell his amazing story. Fortunately, I got a few minutes alone with the young mother, and whispered to her about waterfalls of song. She seemed to understand what I was groping to say: that blessings could be tangible and fall like blossoms on the earth.

What's more, I could read in her eyes that she was saving my story. She would savor it in years to come, as I would. Some invisible bond joined this woman and me, even though we had never met before and would probably never see each other again. But both of us had memorized the same words. In heat, in exhaustion, in pain or pleasure, the same fragments would run through our minds: "Glory to God in the highest;" "a child wrapped in cloth;" "a Savior who is the Messiah." Until then, I had never known that words could be precious stones, treasured like jewels, unwrapped, turned over and over, admired.

In later years, when my children were born, it seemed so familiar; once before, I had seen a baby's fist close over a blanket's rim. I knew how carefully to hold them; I had seen that woman cuddle her child as if he were divine. I cradled visions for them too: beds beneath roofs, freedom from the jeers that had filled my youth. When they were infants, I sang them lullabies as close as I could remember to the angel song. Into those tiny whorled ears, I poured the memory: for you the Savior was born. For you there is good news—an end to the relentless grind; for you, a way out, a potential. I suppose it was fond and foolish, like dusting them with fairy powder, but I clung stubbornly to the promise of peace.

Many years later, I gave in to my grandchildren's pestering. They wanted to see the rabbi everyone was buzzing about. Mostly, I suspect, they wanted the razzle-dazzle of miracles. I had miracle enough in their healthy limbs, reaching and stretching, their bounding energy, the ebony gleam of their hair. Miracle enough their hands in mine as we trekked with sweaty crowds after the teacher.

They scrambled for a spot in front, my little ones, and I followed despite the grumbling mobs. I was close enough to catch the teacher's words, and they snagged the breath in my throat.

"I am the good shepherd." To this crowd, it was like saying, "I am the splendid executioner, or excellent Roman oppressor, or virtuous pimp." Were they snickering at him? They knew perfectly well that shepherds weren't good. Shepherds were outcasts! As he spoke of gates and gatekeepers, of lying down in the opening to the sheepfold, he was describing the grueling work Mark and I had done for the first ten years of our marriage. Was he sanctioning that long fatigue, back-breaking labor, constant complaining about stupid sheep?

A softer tone had crept into his voice, too, as though he saw beneath the annoyance a tender care. It was as if our attention mirrored something of God's mercy. We *had* known each sheep intimately, and had nicknames for each one: Could he be right that God calls us by name? He captured our fears about thieves and marauders, transforming them into an image of a God who would lay down his life for a bumbling beast. It was too good to be true, but I nodded in recognition. I had come full circle; I almost expected to catch a glimpse of that woman in the crowd. If I had, I would have exchanged with her a knowing glance, a look that captured all wisdom.

The children were getting restless; they wanted to see the lame sprint. More talk of sheep just rehashed their grandparents' stories. So I guided them home and gave them fruit and bread to eat. All the while, I hummed an ancient melody. I looked admiringly at my own calloused hands, as if they were braceleted in pearls.

Susanna Today

How do we know what a shepherd woman of Palestine in the first century A.D would have thought? Research has shown that shepherding was often the first job for young women and men of that time, like grocery store sackers or fast food workers today. The job was grim, low-status, poor paying; it doesn't require an enormous leap of the imagination to guess that a young girl would feel trapped in it, or betrayed by an immature husband who had drawn her into the work.

A Midrash technique has long been used to fill in the blank spaces of the Bible by imagining the words between the lines. It is especially helpful as a strategy for women to gain entry and envision their places in texts edited by males. These "traces of feminine presence" give us a means of identifying with our heritage, writes Carolyn Osiek in *Beyond Anger*.[1] Thus after reading the biblical story of the shepherds (Luke 2: 8-20), we can focus on one shepherd, the hypothetical Susanna, and re-create the scenario in terms of what she might have heard, seen, touched, smelled, felt, and thought.

Then, we mine our experience to find parallel patterns. What themes seem to be repeated in our lives? What experiences eventually come full circle, as Susanna's did?

Here is one example. A woman named Claire endured a rather empty existence, with few relationships that nurtured or stimulated her. One day when her office computer was balky, a colleague named Beth offered Claire the use of hers.

Beth was an older woman whose marriage of thirty years had not been easy, but had been richly fulfilling over the long haul. Beth had been ill for several weeks, but still tried to keep her commitments at work. That day, she left early for a doctor appointment, encouraging Claire to use the computer in her office.

Claire accepted the offer and quickly became absorbed in her work. When Beth's phone rang, Claire answered automatically. "Hi honey," said a voice filled with so much compassion that Claire drew a sharp breath. It was Beth's husband; he assumed that Claire was his wife. The mistake was quickly clarified, but the moment made an impression and offered a hope.

Two years later, Claire was talking with a man she loved about a project that would have been disastrous for them both. It took courage to withdraw from the plan, and Claire was vacillating. Then her friend said, "Honey, I wouldn't do it." The sacrifice was as costly to him as to her, but he was trying to help the woman he loved. His first word held the kind of love Claire had heard on the phone.

So as a grandmother, Susanna heard a tone that echoed from her girlhood. Sometimes themes are repeated in our lives as they are in music. But at the time we hear them, we aren't always attuned to their significance. It may take perspective, time, and distance to appreciate a recurring motif. Reflect on or discuss with a friend the themes echoing through your life. What messages have you heard repeated?

- If an exerience such as Susanna's at Bethlehem has had a profound effect on you, recall it now.

- If anything boosted your self-image as Jesus' good shepherd metaphor did for Susanna, savor it now.

- "Mary treasured all these words and pondered them in her heart." What words do you treasure as much as rubies?

FOR REFLECTION OR DISCUSSION

1. The shepherd figures in creche scenes are usually old men. How does it change the picture to imagine a young woman there?

2. Enough sentimental associations have grown up around the good shepherd to cloud the parable's meaning. Religious art sometimes depicts a shepherd so saccharin that any self-respecting sheep would hightail it in the opposite direction.

   When women find themselves treated cavalierly, the sheepish bleats turn to outraged protests. "Baaa? Bah!" More polite people may suppress their anger, but run the risk of "internalizing the oppressor." This is the neat psychological trick Susanna plays on herself when she starts to believe that her work with sheep has made her a smelly outcast. We know that according to rigid Jewish purity codes, her occupation would have marginalized her. It would be unthinkable to resist the clearly defined categories of "pure and holy" vs. "sinful and dirty" in this polarized system.

   Liberation theology has shown us that Jesus came to free people from burdens that reinforce their inferiority. He chooses for himself the status of outcast and uses images that for his hearers would have had evil connotations. Samaritans, for instance, were wicked; the only people who'd associate with shepherds must have lost their sense of smell!

   If possible, overlook the sentimental associations that have grown up around the good shepherd and clouded the parable's meaning. Imagine hearing it as Susanna did, as a metaphor grounded in her experience. What inner chord does it touch?

   While many women resent the implications of being sheep-like, they respond to the image of the friend who lays down a life. That special person knows when we need a joke or a nudge, takes time for the compliment or challenge, restores perspective when we've lost ours: he or she is gift indeed. Then we catch the timbre of the shepherd's voice, drifting over the coffee cups or wine goblets, sounding through a symphony, or rescuing us from depression.

Who has played the friend's role of guardian or gate for you? For whom have you filled this vital role?

3. We don't all get angel choirs. But we do get hints and whispers, flutters so subtle that it takes some reflection to figure them out. "Glory to God in the highest" played in the recesses of Susanna's memory. Ever think about the songs that we hear, the mental Muzak we'd like to tune out, but which persists mysteriously? An advertising jingle, a snatch of hymn, a love song on the radio, a movie theme? Sometimes music lodges so deep in the psyche that it sings forth at odd hours and unexpected moments. For instance, a woman named Kathleen, making a challenging decision and facing a tough transition, heard the Irish-American ballad "I'll Take You Home Again, Kathleen" as though God were reassuring her.

Reflect on or discuss the role music plays in your life; as a form of prayer, sing or play a favorite song.

4. Sofia Cavalletti, a catechist in Rome, founded her process of faith formation on the passage about the good shepherd (John 10:1-18). In *The Religious Potential of the Child*, she describes Maria, a toddler being treated for cancer, who would not speak but only cried. Hearing the parable, Maria was transformed. She kissed her catechist, and sang softly to herself, "He knows my name." Similarly, a Mexican boy facing formidable physical challenges caressed small wooden sheep and assured them, "Do not be afraid; you lack nothing."[2]

What does it mean when a person you respect, perhaps a competent supervisor at work, calls you by name? What does it mean that God calls you by name? How do you recognize God's voice in different timbres?

5.   The ancient ritual of anointing was used to symbolize the holy calling of priests, prophets and kings. A secret formula was used for the precious oils and exquisite perfumes used in the coronation of Queen Elizabeth II. What does this gracious gesture have to do with our daily frenzies, our un-regal routines? Perhaps the answer lies in a broader interpretation of anointing.

When Susanna heard Jesus speak of shepherding, she saw her grinding work in a new light. To continue the anointing analogy, she realized that the sheep oil she could not wash away was a form of holy oil. The stains on her hands were badges of her labor, transformed by Christ into a metaphor for God's care.

Draw a parallel to your own life. Perhaps you don't have blobs of grease on your hands, but the invisible traces of your work linger there. What "holy oils" do you see as you look at your hands? Motor oil, toner, paint, cooking oil, baby lotion, antiseptic, household cleaners, rubbing alcohol, white-out, chalk dust, turpentine . . .

If you like, use the gesture of anointing in prayer, either alone or with another person. Mix perfume with olive oil or baby oil in a small dish. With a generous amount of oil, mark the sign of the cross lavishly on the other person or yourself: forehead, shoulders, hands. If you wish, play soft background music and use the words of the Archbishop of Canterbury, anointing Queen Elizabeth: "Be thy hands anointed with holy oil, be thy breast anointed with holy oil, be thy head anointed with holy oil, as kings, priests, prophets were anointed."[3]

Reflect in silence or in conversation with the other person. How did this ritual help you to see the holiness inherent in your daily routine?

THE OTHER GRANDMOTHER

What of Joseph's mother?
unstoried and unsung,
did she question the
poignant girl, and
hunt her son's resemblance
in the mysterious child?

Or did she, like others in the story,
build from doubt a ladder to delight
in a newborn fist and wobbly head?
She didn't guess that God
might clothe himself in skin,
or stir at her whisper, "Grandson."

2

Magda,

the Wise One

(MATT. 1:1–12)

My gift was not recorded. My companions brought gold, frankincense, and myrrh, but I had a hunch these were no gifts for a child. I had labored long and hard on the cloth I would wrap around the little one, pouring my hope into fabric soft as gossamer. Its colors were the brilliant jade of the first spring leaves against a creamy background, the froth of waterfall.

I had taken up weaving in self-defense, my only nod to "the feminine arts." I never cleaned, stubbornly avoided cooking, and, on principle, refused to do another's dirty laundry. But as I wove, I could tie together the threads of my study. Just as themes interconnected, or one idea illumined another, I could knit colors and blend shades. Sometimes as my hands worked the loom, my mind leaped to connections I might not otherwise have recognized.

But even lovely weaving did not excuse my maverick ways. As a child, my favorite sport had been exploration. My friends soon wearied of my pleas to hike "just a little further," but I was captivated by the potential: around the next bend, a lake might mirror the sun; a field of flowers might shimmer in the wind. So I sought the locales and terrains others rejected, sight unseen. They were happy with their noisy markets, sun-baked streets and familiar cooking smells. I was drawn to shreds of mist snagged in the folds of hills, the fragrance of cedar mingled with wood smoke, and always, always, the distant vista.

Some people branded me a loner, but I didn't mind. I wouldn't have traded my beckoning horizons for their safe niches. The neighbors considered it eccentric for a woman to read as much as I did, but I could dismiss the clucking and burrow into study. It offered as much potential as an unexplored trail or the mauve hills. I have seen the look on my sister's face, when she cannot take her eyes off her new baby. When I am deeply absorbed in reading, I feel the same magnetic pull.

Maybe that's why I was inevitably drawn to a project suggested by one of my colleagues. Everyone else sneered at the idea of an arduous trip with no clear destination. But as he explained his theory and sketched his route, I tingled with anticipation. I've learned to dismiss the worry-warts, so I didn't pay much attention to the voices that whined and warned. The other scholars agreed to take a woman along only because so few men were willing to go. How could I pass up my chance?

It was all fine until we arrived. Unfamiliar vegetation and the inflections of foreign languages have always stimulated me. Years later I could remember tiny details of that journey, probably because every cell vibrated alertly. Serving as look-out, fording a raging stream, tasting exotic foods, I never thought of danger. I only thought, how rich to be alive, guided by a star.

But all the joy was in the journey. What a disappointment when we got there! First there'd been the nasty business with the local king, pesky and probing. Once we'd gotten the information we needed from his scholars, I urged the group to hurry out of there. Enough bowing and scraping in

Herod's palace to last me a lifetime! One of the court flunkies kept leering at me: as though I'd come all this way for a romp in a bug-infested sack with a third-rate politician!

When the star finally stopped, I was reluctant to enter the hovel beneath its glow. Why trade the freedom of the night skies for the stink of moldy straw? When the others persuaded me to enter, I was shocked by the squalor. I grasped my weaving tightly, hesitant to let it touch the muddy floor. When my eyes finally adjusted to the dimness, my heart sank. All these years deliberately childless: must my career reach its pinnacle in a little child?

At least I rose to the occasion. I put on the grandmother-ly look and wrapped the fleece around his satiny arms and legs. As I did, it was as if rigid lines blended; the distinction between giver and gift blurred. The boundaries that had kept me from children ("Stay away from the crazy lady who reads!") dissolved with this child. His mother was accepting in a way my closest relatives were not. She stroked my weaving with reverence; clearly it was her favorite gift.

What's more, she seemed starved for news, and lingered on every word I recounted of our journey. Most of all, she liked hearing about the star, and nodded as though the sign had a certain rightness. She was such a good audience that I embellished my travel tales; anything, I thought, to relieve the dreariness of this shed.

I'll admit I was pleased when the baby's tiny finger curled around my cloth. Other people's children have never held much interest for me, but this one was charming. I didn't mind falling to the ground with the others, although the dra-matic gesture was invented by an overly fervent member of the group. Did the others expect the skin of babyhood to slide off, revealing a rich and powerful king? Did they think his infancy some clever disguise?

I left with many unanswered questions: if only I knew why I'd come so far to see an unimpressive family and their

thoroughly ordinary son. Back to the scrolls, Magda! This
puzzle would take a long time to resolve . . .

Many years later, I heard from a merchant about an especially brutal crucifixion she'd witnessed during her travels. The
soldiers, she said, threw dice for the criminal's clothing. How
banal, I thought at first. Why tell me this sordid tale? But then
she mentioned the color of the cloth: a faded green against a
pearly background. A detail only a woman would notice . . .

It's crazy, I know. Nothing in life ever ends so neatly. But
now in old age, I'm exploring a new field of study. With the
passion of my youth, I am researching the story of this murdered teacher, tracing interwoven threads. I feel the same
excitement I do when my fingers work the loom, seeking
connections, shading one tone into the next. What I've
learned of his teaching joins earthiness and transcendence in
a way no other philosopher approaches. Could there be a connection to the child, the star?

MAGDA TODAY

The Christmas cards picture a cozy tableau: disinfected
camels bow with dignity as the Magi, recently coiffed,
descend from their mounts in a swirl of damask and brocade.
Never mind that these were hardly traveling clothes or that
the animals were probably snarling with hunger and exhaustion. We like our clichés and we like them pure.

Yet the word "magi" is wonderfully vague and could
describe either gender. Seeing their journey through Magda's
eyes gives us a perspective on our own quests. What do we
seek whole-heartedly, despite the voices of doom, the nay-
sayers and cynics? What search do we hold close to the heart?
What quests do we regret giving up? Do we mourn a seeking
self that seems to have sputtered and died from fatigue? What
star pokes or prods or draws us on, even now?

In our day, the wise people, caught up in systemic evils
and dark forces that seem beyond their control, still scan the

skies for a sign of hope. Knowing they cannot stagnate, they journey through unmapped territory at exorbitant cost. But if they do not attempt the exploration, they die. So they summon all their resources—their knowledge, their possessions, their skills—and continue quests that seem to defy logic.

They pursue the star quietly, without fanfare and rockets. They can seem as ordinary as a group of women attending a retreat. Each had been asked to bring some symbol to represent herself in the final prayer service. They sat quietly and patiently through several speakers exploring different facets of spirituality.

But they came fully alive when they brought forth their symbols. From purse and backpack, pocket and briefcase tumbled forth the objects, each one accompanied by a tale. One woman brought a riding spur; another a crocheted sweater. One showed pictures of her grandchildren; another an elaborate spreadsheet. The room filled with a holy hum; the noise level and energy increased; clearly something precious was being spread on the tables and communicated around the circles. The colorful display proved Nathan Mitchell's theory: "For Jesus, conversion is a call to creativity; faith frees the heart for fancy, and salvation always starts as a surprise."[1]

FOR REFLECTION OR DISCUSSION

1. Each "What if?" of history and theology is always intriguing. What if Magda had listened to her critics and said, "Of course, you're right! A long journey would be too hard on a frail woman! My place is here at home." Have you ever caved into popular wisdom and missed an opportunity? Looking back over your life, which chances do you most regret missing?

   On the other side of the coin, when did you take a risk, ignore the skeptics, and seize an opportunity? What part of yourself is crazy enough to follow a star and wild enough to keep exploring, even if the results have been disappointing, even if you're tired or old or just don't feel like it? How has your quest been thwarted or rewarded?

2.   When Magda describes her study, she has clearly found her niche. In that place is her deep center, the channel through which flows the life force. When she operates from that base, she is energized and on target. Clarissa Pinkola Estes in *Women Who Run with the Wolves* defines creativity as "having so much love for something that all that can be done with the overflow is to create." If we do not create, we perish. Or as Estes says, if a woman surrenders the passion of accomplishment, she loses her basic joy. The process of creation brings joy: "her life's blood, spirit-food and soul-life all in one."

"Joy is the kind of feeling a woman has when she lays the word down on the paper just so, or hits the notes al punto, right on the head, the first time . . . it is the kind of feeling a woman feels when she is pregnant and wants to be. It is the kind of joy a woman feels when she looks at people she loves enjoying themselves."[2]

Many of us would envy Magda's single-heartedness. "Yeah," we sigh. "But she didn't have kids. How much could she study with their constant interruptions?" Or we whine, "Easy enough for her. She had the intelligence and the leisure. I'd love to study, but I have to work eight- or ten-hour shifts!" The excuses vary, but they all serve the same function: shutting the doors on sacred creativity, while we self-righteously pursue the mundane and trivial. Writer Toni Morrison says, "We are traditionally rather proud of ourselves for having slipped creative work in there between the domestic chores and obligations. I'm not sure we deserve such big A-pluses for that."[3]

Take your creative pulse. As when we take a pulse on wrist or throat, we may grope for it at first. But when we find it, we know the spot. We feel the surge of blood beneath the skin; we recognize the unique, personal rhythm. We nestle into our niche, our unique form of creativity with the satisfaction of a teenager ploughing into pizza or a nursing baby snuggling into the breast.

"It is the creative potential itself in human beings that is the image of God," writes Mary Daly.[4] If you feel sadly deficient in the creativity department, does some other area of your life compensate? Perhaps in a relationship or in work, do you feel close to God? A runner in the movie *Chariots of Fire* says, "when I run I feel God's pleasure in me." Adapt that statement to fit yourself. Fill in the blank: "When I_____, I feel God's pleasure in me."

3. Magda's weaving brings up the question of gifts. Not simply Christmas or birthday gifts; not necessarily the tangible. Spend some time reflecting on the finest gift you ever received. Bear in mind that it isn't necessarily an item that can be wrapped. It may have been a word, a gesture, a time, an experience, an assurance, a vista. What is the link between gift and giver? What mystery or paradox surrounds the whole notion of gift-giving, so that what is expensive and flashy (gold or myrrh) may be less welcome than something halting and heartfelt? Any parent who's ever received a homemade present, heavy with paste, will recognize this description from *Mama Day* by Gloria Naylor:

    > It was like when a kid labors over a package—the wrapping paper is poorly glued, the ribbon is half tied—and all of his attention is directed towards that space between the hands that offer and the hands poised to receive. It's the gesture that holds the heart of the child.[5]

    Continuing your reflection, what was the best gift you ever gave? What of yourself was poured into it?

How does this reflection on gifts help hone the image of God as gift-giver? What gifts has God placed in your life? Have they been disguised at times, or gift-wrapped and beribboned? Magda would spend a lifetime unwrapping the meaning of the scene in Bethlehem. Which of your gifts have been similar: their significance not immediately obvious or even appealing, but requiring time and thought to understand and appreciate?

4. One way to enter the story is to take different roles in it. Where can you identify Magda in yourself? Perhaps in your discontent—your restless heart that, despite its comforts, hunts for something more, something deeper, some place closer to Christ? Perhaps in the childlike willingness to trust the intuition and bow low in delight? Perhaps in your stubborn perseverance, your sure direction despite the odds stacked against you?

   Shift now to a more painful place, where Herod lurks within. What part of you is hypocrite, mouthing pieties, yet concealing murderous intentions? How do you sabotage your own best self, sneer at reform, and silence your finest instincts? How do you yawn and close your blinds to the star's persistent glow?

   Finally, where are you the child, content in the mother's lap, delighted with the gifts of a gracious God, intrigued by difference and variety? What part of you knows that God delights in you just as you are, and basks in a shining star as the perfect herald of your coming?

5. In *Women Who Run with the Wolves*, Estes explores the significance of human hands.[6] The figures in Mediterranean creche scenes all extend their hands with palms facing the child, as though his light could be absorbed through the hands. Our Lady of Guadalupe showers light through the palms of her hands. One insidious form of terrorism is chopping off a victim's

hands. Sensitive as radar, our hands can read a person through the slightest brush or the quickest hug.

Conclude this chapter by reflecting on your hands. Consider the people they touch, the tasks they do, the messages they send and receive, their potential for healing or hurt, creation or chaos. Look at someone else's hand too. End with a gesture of friendship.

3
Mari,
Ben's Mother

(MATT. 2:16–18)

The children got the feast; the mothers got the heartbreak. I also inherited a question that haunted me the rest of my days: Could I have saved Ben? When I remember that brutal moment, I do not think of my youngest son as "he." I find myself recounting the story directly to "you," as I would tell my little boy a bedtime story.

The rumor had raced through Bethlehem, but it was too horrible to believe. Soldiers slaughtering children who couldn't yet walk? Spears piercing soft baby flesh? Knives slicing infants? Before I could register the news, before I could hide you, that murderous frenzy burst through my gate. In a split second, they found you playing in the yard. Frozen in my memory, you lift your hand to the flashing sword as though they brought a toy. Forever after, you would be two years old, looking up in wonder at the huge soldiers, reaching for the metallic gleam, your throat lifted trustingly to the light. Tendrils of hair curled damply on your neck; your shirt was stained from grapes. That is the picture I carry; the image that followed, I suppress.

How could I ever explain, if I met you again, that you were killed by the murderous wrath of a king who felt he'd been tricked? That there are people so vicious they take out their anger on toddlers? That lacking any tool but a hammer, they treat everything like a nail? That if you had been three or four, or even big for your age, you might have survived? It is my only comfort, that you escaped growing up in a world which has so little respect for those who are small and vulnerable and achingly sweet. It's no place for you, my little one. Perhaps it's a blessing to die young, before the long, insidious corruption takes hold.

A rumor circulated among the mothers that the thugs never found the boy they wanted. Stupid, wasteful men, who have not given birth, who do not know the cost of human flesh, who annihilate every boy under two because one posed a threat. I rake that tortured logic over in my mind, because I do not sleep much. I comb the words of my mother, my husband, and my friends for any consolation, but I find none. They seem to think I'll forget, in time. But no one can deaden the recurring nightmare, or the memory that shadows each day. Nothing will restore your weight in my arms. Years later, I still look into the faces of other children, hunting for your face.

My sister reported the only words that began to close the wound. Oddly enough, this meager comfort came from a criminal. A maniac with delusions of royalty, on his way to crucifixion, he paused to talk to some women from Jerusalem. I remember only one sentence, "Do not weep for me, but for yourselves and for your children." How did he know I'd been doing that almost all my life? I find a strange consolation in that empathy, and hold the words as tightly as your shirt, even after your smell has faded from it. It is all of you that is left.

𝓛♥

Mari Today

The slaughter of the innocents is tersely told in two verses of Matthew's gospel. Yet it is not hard to imagine because the story has been repeated so often in our time. In Rwanda and Mexico, Bosnia and New York City, Rachel still weeps.

One of the most poignant tales of maternal grief comes from Nicaragua, where a catechist told the people: "Mary's son Jesus was disappeared, just like yours. Mary's son was tortured, as your children have been. Mary's son was brutally murdered."

"No. It's different for us," an *abuela* (grandmother) interrupted. "She got to see her son again."

Once a child chortled, smeared jam on clothing, wobbled beneath the sunlit leaves. Now that child is gone. Unable to grasp the harsh reality, we ask the wistful, unanswered question of the grieving mother. Anne Morrow Lindbergh, whose son Charles was kidnapped and murdered at the age of eighteen months, wondered:

> For whom
> the milk ungiven in the breast
> when the child is gone?[1]

The universality of Rachel's weeping was expressed by one of the *madres* who protested the disappearance of their children by a military regime in Chile: "If we find one disappeared one I will rejoice as much as if they had found mine."[2] The ache of the grieving mother transcends national borders. Patricia Donovan lived a comfortable life as a suburban mother; then her daughter Jean was martyred in El Salvador. Speaking to her dead daughter, she records her sense of loss:

> For nine months I carried you under my heart.
> Now you live in my heart forever.
> Sometimes I forget—
> I see a blouse you'd like or a pair of jeans.
> I feel a fist in my stomach—
> There's no one to buy them for![3]

It would insult these women to draw morals from their grief. Yet it would be worse to practice avoidance or denial in their presence. As with a grieving friend, perhaps the best thing we can do is sit with them in solidarity and silence. Reluctant to either ignore or intrude on another's pain, we bow in reverence before it. As we turn from the scene, we carry away a sensitivity that we did not have before. Like people who have viewed the Pieta, we are touched so deeply that we may become gentler, more compassionate.

Within mothers' heartbreaks, we glimpse something of the mystery of God. God said of the beloved people Israel, "How could I part with you? . . . My heart recoils from it, my whole being trembles at the thought" (Hos. 11:8). The mother's loss of her child thus becomes an icon through which we see a little of what we mean to God and the agony of our separation from God.

If a woman who has lost a child could tell us one thing, it might be to cherish the relationships we have. "Your children *live*," she might say. "Why do you become so easily annoyed by their demands? I would give anything for them to bother me again, but my arms are empty. My home is silent."

Mari and her sisters serve as a terrible reminder of life's fragility. Whenever we are tempted to take for granted the people in our care, these women challenge us to remember how precious they are. While we may not bear their terrible torture, we all undergo unique ordeals. We are all called to a sanctity which transcends our differences. In the metaphor of the mystical body, everyone is not a foot or a knee or an eye. We have specific roles to play and purposes to fulfill.

And in one way or another, we all lose our children. If we launch them successfully, they grow up, find their own paths, create lives independent of us. As one mom lamented, sweeping up debris, "First they break your things. Then they break your heart." One of the most difficult tasks facing every parent, teacher, or nurturer is to let the children go, with the serenity of knowing that they never leave God's arms.

FOR REFLECTION OR DISCUSSION

1. Imagine a dialogue between God and Mari. This may take the form of reflection, writing, or conversation with a friend. If you were Mari, what would you say to God? If you were God, what would you say to Mari or the other women in their loss? Remember: This needn't be polite, cocktail party exchange. People who are intimate with each other can shout and rage. The Hebrew people had a long history of fuming at the deity. (If you doubt this, see Psalms 22, 83 and 137.)

2. Continue your own dialogue with Mari, exploring the losses or separations in your life. If the loss is recent or raw, don't force this, or take it slowly and gradually with a trusted counselor or friend. The purpose here is not to rip open a wound, but to enter into the suffering hearts of women and of God.

    Clearly there are no pat answers or easy assurances to offer Mari, any of the women who have lost children, or ourselves. Jesus himself saw into that despair and said, "Blessed are the barren and the wombs that never bore, and breasts that never nursed" (Luke 24:29). Are we "whistling in the dark" when we say that even tragic loss can be transformative? All our stock responses seem to stumble into silence before the death of a child. What in your experience helps you to understand the paradox that Christ's coming was heralded not only by angel song, but also by inconsolable weeping?

3. In *Stations of the Cross: A Latin American Pilgrimage*, Dorothee Soëlle describes a Christian base community in Brazil where landless people gather to pray and protest against large landowners who deny them the basics for survival. When the first child died of malnutrition, they hung a diaper to the crossbeam of their huge wooden

crucifix. Four more diapers had to be hung before the people, aided by the Lutheran church, got a piece of land. The white of the diapers symbolized hope because the families of the children who died eventually gained land in order to live.[4]

The cross hung with diapers is one symbol for the tragedy of Mari and her sisters. What other symbols do you cherish, or could you create for the times when words fail? Sketch, sculpt, sew, write, or design such a symbol through your own creative outlet.

·

MARY READS THE GOSPEL

Were they not like children,
hesitantly bringing their
first drafts, wanting to please
me, I would not have read.

I should be proud, I guess
to see him hero, inspiring text.
But I miss the hidden story
forgotten in blank spaces.

They did not capture
the swish of palms black against
the sunset as we rode toward
Bethlehem, nor Joseph's frown.

The questions screaming in me
louder than the pain, demanding
what creature would emerge from
the cavity of my confusion.

No word about his first yowl,
the infant without herald
announcing himself, no mention
of his satin skin.

The memory in my fingertips
of brushing his hair,
his toddler tummy,
the first steps in sand.

It was not important, then?
That with each birthday, he
grew kinder, deeper. Or the
knife slicing the day he left?

Papyrus is dear; words are
whitewashed. But to erase
the early years silences a
story told only in my heart.

4

Wedding without Wine:

Told in Three Voices

(JOHN 2:1–12)

Lilith

It will be so beautiful. Together beneath the wedding canopy: I in a lacey cloud, Jacob, my golden one. The whole village will envy us: our youth, our eagerness, our bright potential. They will see someone as wonderful as Jacob loving me, bending over me, all his attention inclined toward me. I will rest in his arms and come home.

I have dreamed about our wedding for months. After the ceremony, celebration. Everyone full, happy, forgetting their dull chores and stupid feuds and bitter scarcity for one evening. As they dance, sweat gleams on their faces, feet stomp the floor, glasses of wine vibrate. Motion swirls around us as Jacob and I stand together, the stamen and pistil slender at the heart of the flower. My friends and family hover nearby, smiling approval. They hope that by coming close to our great blessing, some little trace might wear off on them. We do not hear their compliments; we sink into each other. I touch his hand; a cacophony of inner voices stills.

I won't even mind the grumbling of Aunt Eunice. Usually her shrill voice makes something in me curdle. Ever since I was a little girl, she has pounced on every omission, corrected every thoughtless remark, commented on every ripped skirt or dusty sleeve. In each little achievement, she has found the hole. I see her coming and I slam the shutters.

On my wedding day, I will treat her with compassion and calm. I will see through the gaudy clothes and the heavy cosmetics to the lonely child. Sweetly, I will thank her for the awful wedding gift, a vase so ugly I buried it at the back of the closet. I will press more food and wine upon her, good-naturedly stuffing the pillow of her body. Later, Jacob and I will turn to each other and laugh, in that rare moment of understanding when we are alone. Then we will close the door on the whole boring, plodding world; then we shall soar.

Mary

This is the wedding I did not have. It didn't turn out so badly, really. Joseph was magnificent and my son is a treasure I would not trade. But at times like this, some lingering remnant of a girl's fantasy surfaces. I am drawn into the ritual, absorbed in the chanted prayers. In this holy space, the guests are at their finest, filled with lofty emotion, united in good wishes for the young couple who harbor their hopes. This sacred place becomes the locus for all that is best in us; we vest in gracious manners and Sabbath clothing; we soften our raucous voices.

Seeing Jacob and Lilith in their aura of delight, I wonder what it would have been like. Had I not haltingly broken the news to Joseph, had there not been the terrible suspense of several weeks, the bewildered look in my parents' eyes, the hastily arranged marriage, the embarrassment in the village . . . I hear the wedding music and think, "I would have done it this way," or "My ceremony would have been different." Could I too have stood before the rabbi, slim and proud, my husband handsome at my side, my friends like petals surrounding me? It's not often that I think this way; some mysterious chanted chord must evoke the musing.

Murmurs jolt me from dream to reality. Can the wine have run out already? How sad. Their bright bubble popped so soon! Lilith's face crumbles; Jacob's shoulders sag; the music falters; the distress in the room is palpable. The young men talk of replenishing the supply, but it is frantic speculation, groundless boasting. Aunt Eunice moves in for the kill.

The crisis strikes a familiar note. I know what it means to be embarrassed. Far from home, I gave birth in squalor and laid my child in an animal's trough. The memory still vivid, I can empathize.

Still, I hesitate to tell Jesus, so absorbed in conversation that he doesn't hear the hollow clink of empty cups. It is not raw human need: no blood here, no tragedy. Only the throbbing, childish desire to keep celebrating. No doubt, the party could continue. People can survive without wine, just as they can exist without music, birdsong, color. They can grind away at little ruts; they can burrow into drudgery and call it life. All over Palestine, they barely notice the sunset or the stars.

But he would give them more. I know my son, exuberance spilling from him, laughter crinkling the corners of his eyes. He wants everyone to see lilies as he does: clothed in the finery of Solomon's courts. When I think of his rash generosity, I remember Isaiah: "Oh, come to the water all you who are thirsty; though you have no money, come! Buy corn without money, and eat, and at no cost, wine and milk."(Isa. 55:1) He would invite everyone to the banquet with the same gracious disregard for payment. On this unappreciative crowd, their rumbles growing louder, he would pour the abundance of the divine host.

All it would take was one hint. I walked toward him as I had once walked toward Bethlehem, heavily pregnant. I had a vague intuition that I was asking more than a simple favor, that I might be launching something larger. "They have no more wine," I said, and nodded in Lilith's direction, where glow had dimmed to shadow. She was motioning to Michal, her mother; Jacob was muttering urgently to his friends. The tension clouding the room should have been obvious, so I was shocked by Jesus' reply, and wondered: when does "not yet time" slip into the appointed hour? What unimaginable chain of events had I set into motion?

Michal

I could have died from embarrassment. Worse still, eating away at me, was the suspicion that in some nasty mental nook, I had caused the disaster.

I'd been caught up in wedding details for months: planning, delegating, checking, and re-checking. I'll admit it brought a certain energy that the everyday routine didn't have. I was in my element; I'm good at organizing. In a sleepy town like Cana, it's a welcome outlet for a woman.

Wedding preparations also provided a convenient cover for my grief. The thought of Lilith leaving was like an aching wound I must avoid touching. I could not imagine the silent home, the void her going would create. So, girlish again, I got caught up with her in the romance of it all.

When the wine ran out, I realized I'd have to face the yawning hole of an empty life. I could no longer shore up my aging self with a young daughter. I'd been riding the crest of a wave which had fizzled. Now I was stranded. It may have been the loneliest moment of my life.

Because I could not bear the pitying looks of friends or the annoyance of thirsty guests, I slipped into a kitchen alcove alone. There, I peered into the stone water jars as if hoping to read some message in their blue depths. Did some hope glimmer beneath the cool surface? Could I ever be forgiven for this slip, or would the memory of scanty provision and a wedding that ended too soon haunt me forever? What kind of hostess was I, to undercut the celebration at its peak, to drain the exuberance just as it began to build? Had some terrible twist of my mind secretly planned the shortage so Lilith wouldn't leave? Had I sabotaged my other efforts by desperately clinging to her? Would my last ties to Lilith be sliced by her rage at my failure?

I must have been hallucinating, because the waters seemed to color during my monologue. Now you've really lost your mind, I told myself. But I couldn't help scooping a little liquid into my hands. Not since I was a child sipping at a mountain stream have I felt so refreshed. Never have I tasted such flavor, as if the grapes had gathered all the riches of the earth into these burgundy jewels. I drank long and deep, and must admit that I almost sailed over to talk with my old friend Mary.

Over full goblets, she confided that her son was leaving, too. She worried about some mission, well defined in his mind, but vague and dangerous to her. We shared the same ache, but something in the telling calmed us. Or maybe it was the wine. All around me, crusty old men were telling jokes. Ancient enemies were dancing together. Young people were flirting, and it seemed contagious: their parents were looking with misty-eyed kindness on spouses they hadn't talked to since Passover. All my planning and efforts could never have created such warmth for Lilith. People were relaxed, yet seemed to care more intensely. Surely this impossible combination came from another hand than mine.

Ordinarily that recognition would have humbled me, but the remarkable wine seemed to fortify me, too. I was sad but poised when I told Lilith and Jacob goodbye; my kindness to Eunice was easy and unforced. I had looked into a whirlpool where water turned rosy, and had seen wine cascading into pitchers with inexhaustible life. My fretting about the future is set into another frame now: it doesn't go away, but then, it doesn't seem so important either. Arranging every last detail, I know now, is impossible. The most important things are far beyond our control. Instead I savor the present, like each precious ruby of that wondrous wine. I am entranced by the gracious givennesss of the unrepeatable moment. It is so beautiful.

Lilith and Jacob Reminisce

That was only the beginning:
acned and awkward we were then,
embarrassed enough without the wine incident,
indebted to Mary's son for the flow of joy.

Ever since it has been miracle:
touching the shoreline of the other in our sleep,
waking warm beneath our roof,
hoeing the wheat shoots in our fields.

Even the threats brought blessing:
brooding death intensified our life,
illness taught us to nurture the child,
the needy repaid us with Cana's poor gold.

Our union was not singular; we fought
and sulked, sickened like the neighbor folk.
But in every glass of common water,
we tasted hints of garnet-gold.

℘

FOR REFLECTION OR DISCUSSION

1. Looking forward and looking back color the present. Some people say we can have strong hope in the future if we have an equally strong faith in the past. We can face crises, aging and illness, failure and disappointment because we know how graciously God has already acted in our lives. Surely God has more of the same in store! In that spirit, have a glass of wine or grape juice. Toast with the ancient drinking song: "If it's half as good as the half we've known, then here's to the rest of the road!" Continue to sip as you reflect on the rest of these questions.

2. What do you think about these unique characteristics of Jesus' first miracle?

    •   It was prompted by a woman's initiative.

    •   It was not provoked by necessity or tragedy (as later ones were), but by the desire for celebration.

    Male authors tend to see life as a great clash between the cosmic forces of good and evil. In contrast, Mary Belenky and co-authors of *Women's Ways of Knowing* quote a woman: "You know, it's not a battle between the gods that concerns women. Women are concerned with how you get through life from minute to minute. With each little teeny tiny incident—how it can affect everything else you do."[1] How does this insight influence your view of the Cana miracle?

    The Cana miracle speaks profoundly to those who perceive Christianity as a dour business that attracts the prune-faced. The miracle captures instead the spirit of Louise Bogan, who said, "I cannot believe that the inscrutable universe turns on an axis of suffering; surely the strange beauty of the world must somewhere rest on pure joy!"[2] In what ways does this joy enter your life and celebrations?

3. Just as Michal had to separate from Lilith, all women contend with separation in various forms: miscarriage, divorce, job change, disillusionment, moving, retirement, loss of health, the deaths of people they love. How might the water-to-wine miracle help people cope with life's transitions and "necessary losses"? Reflect on the themes of scarcity and abundance in this story, and in your own life.

4. When has Jesus transformed your lifeless waters into the wine that delights? Has the change been gradual or sudden? In what areas do you still need his transforming touch?

5. Recall a time when your vision of social largesse failed to materialize—in other words, a failure as abysmal as Michal's. Yet, you probably still continue to plan, to envision the next birthday or anniversary or wedding or whatever the celebration. What does that perseverance tell you about human resilience?

6. Recall a time when you said to yourself, "That turned out better than I ever could have imagined." What does such an experience tell you of divine grace?

5
Sara,

Peter's Mother-in-Law

(MATT. 8:14–15)

My other daughters married well.
But this one—with his gang of
buddies, smelling like the sea,
carousing as I writhe, feverish.
Not even the grace or sense
to quiet down, or eat at John's.

She houses me to stay the
loneliness (he's often gone).
We chat at twilight as
I braid her hair, stroke
the curly tendrils and
croak her favorite song.

She worries: he left his nets
to dog this rabbi—who'll feed
the family now? I mumble curses
even as the door opens to cure.
A touch brushes my hand
with the coolness of rain.

ℒ♥

U sually, I'm healthy as a horse. But so much has been brewing lately, the tension is fiery as fever in me. First, of course, the death of my husband, then the awful interlude where I not only grieved, but also hung in suspense about my future. Which child would house me? I felt like a rag doll they tossed around—with no say in the matter myself. Secretly, I was glad to move in with Elizabeth; maybe there's a special bond with the oldest daughter. She would be the least likely to make me feel like an extra mouth to feed.

Little did I know about the turmoil in her household. I learned fast, though: not much can be concealed in a three-room house! She was having terrible fights with Peter. Now I'll say up front that he's never been my favorite son-in-law. His big mouth, his rude manners, his fishy smell: ugh. But even though he wasn't my type, he had a certain likable honesty, something forthright and appealing in his bulky stature, his no-holds-barred grin. So it surprised me, at first, the vehemence of this battle raging through their house.

I caught on quickly to the cause: without a nod to Elizabeth, without the slightest thought for his family or his fishing, Peter had decided to up and follow Jesus. The nerve! Whatever could possess a man, to leave his livelihood? Were his children supposed to fend for themselves? It put a huge burden on Elizabeth: three little ones to feed and her husband running after some rabbi.

Another undercurrent swirled as well. As I said, I can guess what my daughter thinks before she says it. Gradually I figured it out: Elizabeth yearned to follow Jesus, too. "Oh, Mama," she breathed in an unguarded moment. "Everything Jesus says is wondrous. He offers people a new way of treating each other, and he shows them how to be kind. When he talks about lilies and sparrows and yeast, the stuff we pass by every day, he gives them another layer of meaning. He sees ordinary things in a new dimension!"

Then I understood what the argument was really about. Elizabeth was pulled in two directions. Much as she wanted to follow Jesus with Peter, she had a nursing baby and two toddlers to care for. Her frustration with Peter may have started in the loss of an income, but escalated with every word of Jesus that she missed. Rumors of miracle just added fuel to the fire.

"Why can't Peter report back to you? Can't he tell you what the teacher says?" I blundered. Then I saw the disappointment wash over her face, as I clicked onto her mental list of People Who Don't Understand. I should've known: Peter may have had his gifts, but remembering an image or a nuance wasn't his strong suit. I could imagine the pained look on his face as he groped to remember: "Well, I think he said something about salt. And lamps and baskets. I'm just not sure how that all went together. Sorry, honey!"

Then Elizabeth would turn away hungry, to change another diaper or scale another fish. No wonder she was seething. She could have absorbed the delicate peach tones that tinged the clouds at sunset; she knew the infinite varieties in a lake's surface: the palette shifting from pewter in the early morning to mauve at twilight. Now she was cheated of words that poured over the crudest fishermen as they loaded their ropes and gear or swilled their beer. She who would have vibrated to the most delicate grace note was missing the concert.

If she hadn't been so sensitive, she probably could have left the children without a qualm. But I watched her tuck them in at night; I saw how deftly she brushed their tangled hair; I knew how gently she eased their arms from their sleeves. She could no more have told them good-by than she could have amputated her own leg. She told me once, brave and defiant, that *she* could rub their soft skin; *she* could tell them stories: what more did she need?

But at another level, she yearned for Jesus with an intensity she could neither bury nor disguise. When Peter was gone for a long stretch, the desire ate away at her. She became irritable with the children; even in her garden, she was restless. I was furious with Peter, I was enraged at Jesus, and I wasn't too happy with myself. Why couldn't I help Elizabeth? I'd survived other crises with her; why did I feel so inept with this one? I was helpless to intervene; even though I'm older than God, I'd never dealt with anything like this before.

So, stupidly, I got sick. It was the last thing Elizabeth needed then. But the more I berated myself, the worse it got. What was burning within me: genuine illness or piled-up annoyance? I didn't much care: my eyes aching, my throat parched, all I wanted to do was curl into hot oblivion.

Then a commotion at the door swirled through my dreams. Peter loud and boisterous, expecting a welcome home; Elizabeth trying to quiet the men; the baby shrieking; a voice I didn't recognize, asking for *me*? Before I knew what was happening, a hand touched mine and drew me out of the fiery spiral.

Let me set one thing straight. When Matthew said I got up and waited on them, everyone assumes I fell all over myself cooking up a storm for Jesus and his friends. To tell the truth, I was still a little woozy, and felt weak through the rest of his stay. What kind of woman leaps out of a sick bed to feed strangers?

But I will say this: He listened closely to my concerns about Elizabeth. While we talked, some mysterious force surged in me, some conviction that I was more than a dusty pot shoved to the back of the shelf. I also began to understand the mystery of the mother–daughter connection. Elizabeth and I chose the same colors, laughed at the same things, had similar mannerisms. If we were so alike, it gave me a glimmer of what Genesis meant when God created humans in the divine image. Just as Elizabeth was like me, so I was like God. Maybe I could be more active, more creative in resolving her dilemma.

As I emerged from the fever, I saw my role clearly. I was the only one Elizabeth would entrust with those children; I was the only one who could persuade her to leave them for a few days. "They'll be fine with me," I assured her, even as I sewed a sling for the baby. It was a makeshift contraption, but he was happy as a clam in it, snuggled close to her.

The day Elizabeth set off with Peter to follow Jesus, she held her chin a notch higher. The baby secure on her back, she walked with a jaunty step I hadn't seen since her wedding. As she said good-by to me and the children, she waved with a freedom I hadn't noticed in years. As for "she ministered unto them," I'm enjoying the grandchildren immensely, knowing how Elizabeth appreciates having them safe with me. They're proud of themselves, too, helping with my cottage craft that brings in a little income. Young mothers are buying baby slings as fast as I can sew them.

SARA TODAY

Okay, maybe it's too simple, and the dilemma of Elizabeth, Sara, and Peter wasn't solved as easily as the story suggests. Elizabeth may have never gotten the chance to follow Jesus. Perhaps she poured what she knew of his teaching into her children's hearts. Her husband got all the publicity, but she made a quiet contribution that was just as important. Does that rationale sound too much like the condescending rhetoric used for too long to "keep women in their place"? Does this scenario make Elizabeth less holy than Peter?

How would you continue and resolve the story? The answer is important, because the dilemma persists. In our own lives, we try to answer the questions raised here. Many women probably envy the freedom of the first disciples (and of some subsequent followers) to simply pull up stakes and immediately follow the itinerant preacher. They empathize with the women who must have told Jesus, "I want with all my heart to follow you—can you wait 'til I find someone to watch the children?" Were the children that Jesus blessed the offspring of women who dragged them along on their personal quests? Was Jesus aware of their inner struggles when he established a firm policy of "Children Welcome Here"?

How does Elizabeth's conflict play out today? Do our churches still post unwritten signs, "Kids Keep Quiet"? Do women still feel schizophrenic, torn between their own desires for spirituality, and the incessant demands of their families? Is the peace and quiet conducive to prayer an unreachable state for most women?

Wendy Wright suggests in *Sacred Dwelling* that the women who heard the radical call of Jesus did not drop everything and walk away as the men did. This new and powerful love entered their hearts along with all their other loves, not displacing their affection for spouses, families, and friends, but bringing it new depth and richness. Jesus' coming reshaped and enlarged their capacity for love.[1]

Sherry Anderson and Patricia Hopkins, authors of *Finding the Feminine Face of God* point to spiritual forefathers who couldn't quest for God unless they were stripped of allegiances to family and home through severe testing. But what about women, who *make* homes rather than leave them? Their research found that for the most part, women who outgrew old concepts and ideals did "leave home," but not in the physical sense. Rarely did they sever ties with those they loved. Instead, they found their connections with the sacred at home, by moving deeper into what they already had.[2]

Perhaps this is what Matthew means by the puzzling statement, that as soon as the fever left her, "she got up and began to serve him." The suggestion that a barely recovered woman would cook for a stranger has an uncomfortable note that realists would characterize either as "codependency" or the delusion of an arrogant author.

Another perspective might be that Sara's gratitude to Jesus spilled over into service to her family. As her insight on what it meant to be made in God's image took shape, she began to recognize an overlooked or forgotten part of herself. Her syllogism "Just as Elizabeth is like me, so am I like God," gave her a power on which women today draw.

It also works both ways, connecting a woman not only to her daughter, but also to her own mother. Wright speaks of her connections: "through my mother and her mother, I am linked to the tuck and pat, the abstracted hum of women who died long before I was born. Their tenderness yearns out over the crest of a melodic line, spanning years and miles to bless me and to bless, through me, my children."[3] An intricate weave connects the generations and threads us to God.

FOR DISCUSSION AND REFLECTION

1. Sara gets a second chance, and her healing is as much mental as physical. When have you had a similar experience, a shift in outlook so significant it changed your behavior? For a few minutes, sit with that transformation; savor it in retrospect. What images, colors, or feelings arise? Give some expression to your response.

2. In all the Gospel accounts, we never read about Peter's wife. The only hints come in this vignette about her mother (Matt. 8:14–15; Mark 1:30–31). To even consider her existence must be mildly subversive; although the church has known for centuries that Peter had a wife, she is shrouded in silence. Many years ago, Virginia Woolf asked, "What if Shakespeare had a sister?" As she imagined the bard's feminine counterpart, she hypothesized that the woman would have committed suicide because her gifts were so unappreciated and underutilized.[4]

   So what of Peter's spouse? Use a Midrash technique to fill in the details. Imagine Elizabeth: her life before and after Peter met Jesus and turned the household upside down to follow him. The Gospels paint Peter as an outspoken, blundering man—with a few moments of grace. What was it like to be married to him? What was Elizabeth's relationship to Jesus? Do you think it's inevitable that when one person stands in the limelight, another must play the behind-the-scenes role? Is that situation unjust, or does it contain some saving grace?

3. Now place yourself imaginatively in the role of Sara, Peter's mother-in-law. If it helps, imagine having high fever. Then feel Jesus' touch on your hand, cooling the furnace of your disease. How do you feel as the illness dissolves and the ache fades? What does he say to you? What do you say to him?

4. Have you ever been in the embarrassing position of rejecting a person (either internally or outwardly), then receiving a large favor from him or her? What insight did you gain from that experience? What part of yourself do you tend to reject? What might you learn from befriending that neglected area of your personality?

5. Here is a collage of quotes about healing, or about sharing a problem that cannot be immediately healed. Spend time reflecting on the ones that energize you.

   • "Love is the resetting of a body of broken bones."[5] — Thomas Merton

   • "*La Loba* sings over the bones. This is our meditation practice as women, calling back the dead and dismembered aspects of ourselves . . . Within us is the potential to be fleshed out again as the creature we once were. Within us are the bones to change ourselves and our world. Within us is the breath and our truths and our longings—together they are the song, the creation hymn we have been yearning to sing."[6]—Clarissa Pinkola Estes

   • "Many of life's problems and challenges have no answer; one can only live with and through them. Problems and challenges, however, can be faced and lived through with more peace and resilience if people know they are not alone."[7]—William Barry

- "It is in the shelter of each other that people live."[8] —Peig Sayers

- "The maxim of illusory religion runs: `Fear not; trust in God and [God] will see that none of the things you fear will happen to you'; that of real religion, on the contrary, is `Fear not; the things that you are afraid of are quite likely to happen to you, but they are nothing to be afraid of.'"[9]—John Macmurray

- With deportation to a Nazi concentration camp imminent, Etty Hillesum wrote, "That is all we can manage these days and also all that really matters: that we safeguard that little piece of you, God in ourselves. And perhaps in others as well. . . . There are, it is true, some who . . . are putting their vacuum cleaners and silver forks and spoons in safe keeping instead of guarding You, dear God . . . They forget that no one is in their clutches who is in Your arms."[10]

6. In your imagination, accompany Elizabeth and Sara as they stroll through St. Peter's Basilica in Rome. Probably, they admire the art, the sculpture, the grandeur and scope. Most likely, they are also baffled: where in that vast edifice is any commemoration of them, or the parts they played in the early Christian church? Either try to explain why they are missing, or create a fitting commemoration. Complete this sentence through art, music, mime, writing, or discussion, "If I had built this church, I'd include this altar to Peter's wife: . . . "

6

Leah,

Wife of Jairus

(MARK 5:21–24, LUKE 8:40–56)

He gets the credit,
but who gauged the mounting fever?
Whose stomach wrenched, whose
fingers gripped glacier as
her wrist turned flaccid? Activity
a facade, I memorized her face.

Silly man patted my hand and reassured
me kids snap out of these things
(the resilience line). My voice
gentled each syllable of her name, but
in the corners of her moan I heard
the knell and said "Get Jesus."

He stalled. How could Mr. Synagogue
fawn before the wandering rabbi?
I saw her sheets twisting to shrouds
and with fist in my voice roared
"I will not lose my child
to stupid arrogance. I'll go myself."

Instead of ultimatum, he heard
the faltering of her breath.
A man who had not run in seven years
turned cheetah. He was too late.
Burying my head in her chest
I cursed the cloying flutes

and his delay. I held her fiercely 'til
I heard commotion and *"Talitha, kum."*
Were the words for her or me? Weeping
like orphaned child, I know only that
we rose together. I can contain this
joy no more than I could host the grief.

My confusion camouflaged, I
find her bread, a drink for the master.
Who am I to question miracle?
But stubborn, I would contradict him:
I know how my daughter sleeps and
she was not asleep.

A Guided Meditation

If you are willing, travel in your imagination to another time and space. The year is 32 A.D. You are a woman named Leah, living in a warm climate; palm trees dust the horizon. Your home is comfortable, a salmon-colored stucco. It is built around an inner courtyard where your garden flourishes. In the morning and evening, you enjoy the coolness there, seeing your almond trees and flowers in purple and dusky pink.

Your husband Jairus is a synagogue official, a scholarly man who sometimes seems preoccupied, but your marriage of twelve years is usually calm and happy. For the last nine years, your life has been wrapped around your daughter Rachel. You love seeing her in the morning with her hair sticking straight up, her barely opened eyes; preparing the fruits and dates she likes to eat; watching her play with her friends.

Now she is critically ill. Her wracking cough is alarming; her fever mounts precariously high. As you hold her hand, the wrist seems flaccid; her color is a dangerous yellow. Your husband downplays your concern and ignores your pleas.

"*Do* something!" you insist for the hundredth time. You are full of rage, as he becomes the target for all your frustrations about Rachel.

He stalls. She coughs. You've had it. "What about that rabbi, Jesus?" you prod Jairus. "My sister said he does miracles. Surely you know him. Don't they talk about him in the synagogue?"

His scorn is no surprise. "Some maverick? How could he help our Rachel?" She tosses in bed; you imagine her sheets becoming shrouds.

"I'll go to Jesus myself," you warn him. You have already calculated his disdain. That move would represent the ultimate indignity: a rabbi's wife running after some itinerant preacher, asking him a favor? But you look at Rachel's closed eyes, and you don't care about status.

Jairus does not seem to hear the ultimatum. Instead he hears Rachel's breath falter as she twists in bed. He feels her forehead; without a word, he leaves the house.

"Where has the wretched man gone?" you wonder, holding Rachel fiercely, sponging her with water, stroking her hair. Wherever he searches now, he is too late. Helplessly, you call her name, but she is beyond the furthest reaches of your voice. You bury your head in her chest.

If you have a child or grandchild, or love another person deeply, pause now. Reflect on what the death of the beloved might mean . . .

The next thing you hear is commotion, and the words, "*Talitha, kum,*" little girl, get up. You have been as lost as an orphaned child, weeping inconsolably. Your tears have soaked Rachel's gown; she lies still. Her strange peace contrasts with your turmoil. Yet the words seem addressed to you both. The child within you looks up in hope to the stranger at the bedside. Rachel stirs. You rise together.

Joy explodes within you like larks ascending into cobalt skies. You wonder if your heart can contain this elation; you have not felt so deeply grateful since you learned you were pregnant with Rachel. You hug her as though you will never let go. You embrace Jairus, all resentment forgotten. And with both hands, you grasp the hands of Jesus. What do you want to say to him? Pause for a few moments of silence. Imagine yourself talking to him . . . Imagine how he might respond . . .

Remain in dialogue with Jesus for a few more minutes. Then begin to let the images fade . . .

When you are ready, begin to become aware of this place. Hear the sounds of this room. Feel your feet on the floor. Take a few minutes of silence, then share with another person or write whatever you wish.

FOR DISCUSSION AND REFLECTION

1. Of the three accounts of this story (Mark 5:21–24, 35–43; Matt. 9:18–26; Luke 8:40–56), Mark and Luke mention the mother's presence. How does imagining the story from her perspective change it for you?

2. Both Leah and Jairus wanted to save Rachel, but they took different approaches to the same goal. Name the tensions between Leah and Jairus. Which of these still enter into your relationships with other people?

3. Paradoxically, the death of a child orphans the parent. Broaden the image of "child" to include your dreams and hopes. Which of these have died from procrastination, lack of energy, money, support, or time? Which undeveloped project or unborn dimension of yourself do you mourn?

4. What child within you needs to be encouraged to rise up and emerge? Is it a spirit of play, wonder, daring? Or do you need to spend more time healing the child who has been hurt and still weeps?

5. What emotions did you discover within yourself when you spoke to Jesus after the miracle?

7

Feeding Five Thousand

—and Me, Raissa

(JOHN 6:1-15)

I wasn't counted, but I ate my unofficial fill.
I played my part in seeding this desert,
channeling the silvery cascade of fish.
Who do you think brought the baskets?

The children just chewed, smiles crumb-smudged.
Unimpressed by murmurings of miracle or gourmet reviews,
they swallowed a lavish memory, extravagance
overflowing the rationed plates of other days.

Another hunger soothed by the reverence in hands
touching loaves as if they were ivory
blessing bread as if an empress dined
lifting us like crystal goblets to each other's lips.

Afterward, gummed crusts gathered with care
bent grass imprinted with our sheen.
We left plucky as a people dared, fiesty, fueled,
yeasty, dangerous. Almost as if we count.

"**D**on't forget your lunch!" I called after the swirl of dust that was my son Ephraim. I thrust a couple fish, some barley loaves into his grubby hands, then grabbed the baby and my basket. This trip wasn't my idea, I grumbled all the way there. I didn't look forward to standing on the fringes of the hot, smelly crowd, feeling discounted and dull. I could barely remember a time before children when my edges were sharp, my skin taut. For the umpteenth time, I followed Ephraim, a daredevil who would push his way forward, while I fumbled with the fussy baby on the edge.

What was the commotion up front? Around me, people were grumbling about the heat and their hunger. Was Ephraim safe? If I could find him, maybe we could escape the chaos. As I stood on tiptoe, peering toward the teacher whom I couldn't even hear, my worst fears materialized. There stood scrawny Ephraim, grinning, handing over his miserable lunch. Before I had a chance to be embarrassed, neighbors recognized him, and shoved me forward. Wanting only to rescue Ephraim, I ignored their rude jeers.

But I was too late. The teacher had taken the food into his hands, touching it with extraordinary reverence. You'd have thought those loaves were gold, and the fish scales, delicate lace. I stopped in my tracks; the baby in my arms quieted. I couldn't hear the teacher's words, but the crowd started buzzing with news. Suddenly, the sun gleamed on a silvery cascade of fish and tawny mounds of bread.

That wasn't the only transformation. I know these people: on better days, we consider ourselves pond scum. We're un-combed and unwashed; in the heat, we reek. We can count on one hand the compliments we've heard. Not much beauty in our brutish days. But this Jesus treated us like we were somebody. He and his friends served that meal as though we dined at the palace in the cool shade of marble columns. And we responded in kind.

The laughter bubbled, the conversations swirled in this green oasis. Men who hadn't looked at their wives except in drunken lust bent over them with tender concern. People who kicked their kids more often than their dogs were asking if they wanted seconds. Breaking the bread, we admired its texture and inhaled its fragrance. We who usually shoveled it down ate with delicacy and poise. I wouldn't have been surprised if music drifted over the scene.

Even the invalids were included. The other women and I added the little food we'd brought, and those who couldn't remember their last meal consumed a lavish banquet. We gathered the leftovers in a daze of satiety, filling our baskets again. Some accountant types, those who'd seated us in rows, tried to count the men, but of course they missed the point. This rare grace didn't fit onto a ledger sheet. For a moment there, our wretched scarcity blossomed into abundance. We forgot our grating poverty in sweeping gestures of graciousness. Our ancestors would have said the desert bloomed.

No longer blunted nor numb, I lifted my chin a notch and smoothed my hair. For an hour, I was the queenly hostess. After all, I had packed that lunch.

RAISSA TODAY

With multiple demands upon her, Raissa probably tossed together Ephraim's lunch while she fed the baby and cleaned up the breakfast, giving it little thought at the time. Yet Jesus' touch transformed her unconscious task. He fed not only the physical hunger, but the deeper need for blessing, meaning and praise. She played her part in miracle.

After the meal, Jesus directed that the fragments be gathered, "so that nothing may be lost." With multiple demands on time and energy, most contemporary women feel fragmented and distracted. How can we bless our apparent chaos and draw abundant life from it?

Jesus' directive suggests that in prayer we can lift the fragments to him. If he gathers the pieces, nothing of value is lost. Just as the collage or quilt joins scraps into beautiful unity, so his broad arms embrace everything.

Women who anguish over distracted days and divided hearts may be affirmed by this passage from *Composing a Life* by Mary Catherine Bateson:

> Women have been regarded as unreliable because they are torn by multiple commitments; men become capable of true dedication when they are either celibate, in the old religious model, with no family to distract them, or have families organized to provide support but not distraction, the little woman behind the great man.
>
> But what if we were to recognize the capacity for distraction, the divided will, as representing a higher wisdom? Instead of concentration on a transcendent ideal, sustained attention to diversity and interdependence may offer a different clarity of vision, one that is sensitive to complexity, to the multiple rather than the singular. Perhaps we can discern in women honoring multiple commitments a new level of productivity and new possibilities of learning.[1]

FOR DISCUSSION AND REFLECTION

1. How do you respond to Bateson's idea that the complexity of modern life may be an opportunity, a "higher wisdom" rather than a frustration? Imagine one day in your life. How does the pull of many demands draw you out of being overly self-conscious?

    To ritualize the idea that many separate pieces are holy, make a braid—either in reality, in your imagination or on paper—from ribbon, cord, hair, or fabric strips. How do the three strands strengthen the whole? What themes do the three strands represent in your life? How do they come together?

2. Slowly and deliberately, take a piece of bread, break and
    bless it, share it with a friend if possible, and eat it.
    Savor the taste, the texture, the fragrance. The gesture
    has long roots and archetypal overtones. What does it
    mean to you? Contrast this intentional process with the
    "fast food fix."

3. When Jesus chose meals for some of his most important
    revelations, he stood squarely in a long Hebrew tradi-
    tion. Macrina Wiederkehr writes in *A Tree Full of Angels*:

    > The Hebrew people took quite seriously the event of
    > eating together. They did not lightly break bread with
    > one another. Would that we could be a bit more care-
    > ful about eating together, remembering that when we
    > eat together we proclaim that we are friends and can no
    > longer betray one another![2]

    Reflect on your own style of eating. Has dinner
    with conversation become an "endangered species" in
    your household? Is it too old-fashioned for families to
    share themselves and their stories as well as their food
    at the end of the day? Do you "graze" or drive-through
    frequently? Is there room in your week for a variety of
    dining styles?

    How would you respond to this quote from James
    Dunning in *Echoing God's Word*?

    > We trivialize meals with fast food, convenience food,
    > junk food and meals on the run. But Jesus and his
    > church knew that meals created a holy bond between
    > host and guest. "To take a meal with another was to
    > offer the right hand of fellowship in the deepest sense
    > of the word."[3]

    What parallels do you see between the multiplication
    of loaves, the eucharistic meal and meals in your own
    household?

4. If we are fortunate, we have known people who touched us as Jesus touched Raissa. His influence turned a frazzled mother into a regal hostess. Knowing him, she came alive. She became her finest self.

    •   Name the people who have had that effect on you. If possible, get out pictures of them and linger over them. If they are still alive, write or phone them.

    •   Under your touch, some people have blossomed. Acknowledging your influence isn't an ego trip, but a form of praise, for you have acted as God's channel into their experience. Again, linger lovingly over their pictures. Recall moments of grace in the relationship. If possible, contact this person, with renewed reverence for the mysterious dynamic between you.

8

Anna,

the Adulterous Woman

(JOHN 8:1–11)

You don't know the whole story. For starters, you don't know my husband. Just because I'm his property doesn't mean I have to like him. I tried at first, but quickly grew to dread his heavy step at night, his attitude of owner-ship. It was lonely, with the other women simpering over him, no one I could talk to. I felt caged: my youth leaching away, my figure thickening—would I grow old before anyone ever told me I was beautiful?

I wondered if the women giggled behind their hands about a pleasure I had never felt. One or two seemed to be more than the furniture in their homes, the fixtures in their husbands' beds. But to me they spoke a foreign language. Inexperience was the only way I could explain my lack of interest in the sex that pulsed like undercurrent through our jokes, that swirled like dust around our marketplace.

Nor do you know my lover. Just the memory stirs some-thing too deep to describe: so I will say only that he walked with the grace of trees bending in the wind; that on his arms the hair gleamed golden in the sun; that he awakened long-ings in me which I'd ignored so long, I thought they were dead. When we talked, the air between us sparkled; I did not know that anyone could listen so carefully, could hold me as though I were fragile. He told me I was lovely; he stroked my hair with reverence, came to me as to an altar.

Know this too: we were first friends. When he walked beside me, we fit together. In many ways, we meshed. When we were separated, the ache became physical. My yearning just to touch the man, just to have five minutes alone with him became fierce. In my head, I knew that making love with him would break every law in the whole Mosaic book. But my body didn't get the message. My shoulders leaned toward him, my skin tingled in his presence, my bumping into him was not an accident. As the light kindled in his eyes, that look mirrored mine. Together we fed some force spiraling beyond the social code. Perhaps I drank poison, but it tasted sweet and I was thirsty. Is happiness always so bittersweet, virtue always so empty?

You don't know what a good girl I'd been, 'til now. Silent and resigned, I had gone like a puppet to the husband my parents selected. They had pulled my strings during childhood, then turned the handle over to my husband. I had settled for that mindless security, accepted that narrow box as my lot. Naive and vulnerable, I simply suppressed my yearning for more.

Do not think that the ecstasy, when it finally came, was without cost. I paid dearly, with even our finest moments together tearing me apart inside. The morning that I saw shadows at the window, I knew a long-delayed bill had finally come due. Pay up, I told myself. I could almost welcome the relief of stones raining on my head. I had overreached; I should be reduced to size; I had stolen joy. They could not hurl an accusation harsher than those that rang from within.

When they dragged me into the square, the veins throbbing in their temples, their faces flushing burgundy, they all wore the rage of my husband. He was there, too, egging on his friends, fueling the fury that robbers could so easily steal their property, surfacing the fear that *their* wives might take that disastrous step beyond the pale. Weaving in and out of the men in the crowd, the women were almost as lurid, trying to glimpse one who might stir some latent desire, who had acted on urges they buried long ago.

The charge—"caught in the very act"—sounded redundant. Their voices emphasized "very," but one look at me, and anyone would know: the high color on my cheekbones, the blush climbing my neck, the thin damp film on my thighs, the taste of him on my lips, the smell of him on my skin. I clutched a flimsy cloth to cover my nakedness, knowing it was futile.

The mob leered with envy; they weighed the stones in sweaty palms. They itched to fling their rocks, but I wanted that barrage even more—the hard granite quelling my body's demands; the pain my penance; the oblivion a welcome end to my torment. The only way I could stand before them was knowing that within minutes, I could sink into a bloody puddle, beyond the reach of their probing eyes. Something about stoning had a bizarre appeal to my sense of justice. I had had one splendid gift (his face before me); I would take my punishment.

How dared this rabbi interrupt a predestined drama? "Quit fiddling in the dirt, and let them get on with it!" I almost pleaded. Yet I was fascinated with his squiggles in the sand, as though those spirals traced some unfinished pattern in my life. The paths sketched by his fingers did not end there in the square; they beckoned on and on. What new direction was he suggesting?

When this Jesus straightened up, he had a familiar grace, a gesture I had loved, a voice like one that had called me beautiful. I steeled myself against it, terrified that someone might awaken me again. I belonged on the ground, the pulp beneath the boulders, not standing erect and holding conversation with a teacher!

But that is precisely what happened. They shuffled off grumbling, some still fingering stones, and we were left alone. Poised in that moment, the boulders would have been easier than the call to freedom. "Don't sin again," he said, but he never spelled out what it meant. Which was sin: returning to my lover, or to my husband? Which was justice: denying my newborn self, or honoring a moral code that our ancestors had venerated for centuries? I wanted closure; I got an open gate. I wanted certainty; I got a hint. I wanted death; I got life.

During my long walk from the square, one image came to mind. I remembered the dry bones rattling in Ezekiel. Maybe because flesh had recently become dear to me, I could see the bones joining, the sinews inching over them, the skin knitting a cover. And then I remembered: the spirit of God brought the skeleton to life. Yahweh had breathed, "O my people!" and I recognized the yearning in God's heart. God's voice trembled with compassion, understanding why we limped so painfully, knowing the reasons for our fears and fatigue. "I am going to open your graves . . . I will put my spirit within you, and you shall live," said the Lord. Had I today heard an echo of that promise, the same timbre of kindness in Jesus' voice?

Where would I go next? I know only that I walked with confidence, for Jesus had trusted me with the decision. He treated me as the equal of the Pharisees and scribes, inviting us *all* to start afresh. As Isaiah said, a way opened in the wilderness; streams turned the desert green.

ANNA TODAY

The genius of the Gospel is the unanswered question. Just as Jesus refused to give a clear-cut solution, but called Anna to work out his directive in her life, so he poses the same frustrating dilemmas in ours. Conflict can then become a gate to new life or a bridge to greater freedom. Our current problem may not be a sexual issue, but it's bound to be something. What debate rages in the places below consciousness? What issue surfaces in sleepless nights? What constitutes the 3 A.M. dilemma?

The Gospel story opens vistas beyond our comfort zones, plants us in uncharted territory. Knowing how Anna interpreted that writing in the sand is probably less important than reading the text Jesus writes in our lives. Where are our energies now? What reluctance do we have about writing our futures? Where is our terrible freedom calling us next? Along uncertain paths and rocky roads, who shows us glimpses of God's face? For what do we dare to hope? What part of us keeps stubbornly resurrecting, when we'd rather leave her cozily entombed?

QUESTIONS FOR REFLECTION OR DISCUSSION

1. As Anna sets out on a new path, she carries in her heart two talismans: The image of bones coming to life (Ezek. 37:1–14) and the words, "I am about to do a new thing: now it springs forth, do you not perceive it? I will make a way in the wilderness and rivers in the desert" (Isa. 43:19). Typically, she draws on her rich tradition for support. What snatches of poetry or song, stories, quotations, symbols, or images do you turn to for strength in times of transition or decision? Collect a collage (actual or imagined) of these treasures. Hang it on your wall or hold it in your heart. What has made these touchstones so precious?

2. In the context of this Gospel, Dom Helder Camara, Bishop of Recife, Brazil, asks, "Ought we to rate sexual sins as worse than sins against compassion?"[1] While we all know how we'd *like* to answer that question, how would you answer it truthfully? In practice? In theory?

To what extent do we need to undergo an experience like Anna's in order to grow in compassion? We may think that only primitive peoples controlled others by sexual definitions, but how does that practice continue today? How might our churches or communities change if we put into practice an honest "no" to Camara's question?

3. Forgiveness, especially of ourselves, is never easy. Yet Jesus forgives the scribes and Pharisees who viciously attack and humiliate Anna, offering them the same new life he holds out to her. If we ever doubt whether forgiveness is possible, we need only look into the face of Jesus. Close your eyes and take a long look now. Ask him for the grace to forgive. What does he answer?

4. Writing in *The Catechist's Connection* (April 1995), Phyllis Calvey recommends a "gospel in your pocket." Choose a small, smooth stone to carry in your pocket. When you are tempted to judge or criticize another, touch the stone and hear Jesus saying, "Let anyone among you who is without sin be the first to throw a stone" (v.7). Some people will start to say something unkind, touch the stone, and leave the sentence unfinished.

5. The Sufis tell the story of a prince who asked a woman the price of a rug she had made. She replied, "One hundred rupees." Shocked, the ruler inquired, "Why would you sell such beautiful weaving so cheaply?" She answered in surprise, "Because until now I did not know there were any numbers higher than a hundred."

   Because of her cultural conditioning and background, Anna also underestimates herself. Like the Sufi woman, she probably doesn't count much beyond one hundred. She sees stoning as an acceptable, even welcome punishment for adultery. We may be tempted to dismiss this as the problem of illiterate people in under-developed countries. But to some extent, we share the same conditioning. What disappointments or negative messages have caused you to undervalue yourself or to simply quit trying?

When Anna met her love, her self-esteem soared. What people or experiences have helped you to see yourself in a more positive light? Do you think we love others for the people they are, or do we love the person we become with them?

9

Miriam's Threshold

(LUKE 7:11–17)

Behind, the snug huts of Naim
bracketed her former life:
wells and maize, violet mornings,
sills crossed routinely
and precious as pulse,
her son at the door.

Ahead, a terrain bleak as bone
an endless plain without oasis
where his sandals would not
carve scallops in the dust.
The sad procession paused,
her lifted arch hovered and

Light as wing, a hand brushed
the bier like water melting clay
into supple form. Confluence
of her held breath, his art:
a boy's skin colored
a toe twitched.

> The scene a gauzy scrim
> for a boulder fractured,
> shrouds cast aside, and
> another mother pivoting
> from silent zone to
> a room electric with voice.

Bent beneath the double blow, bearing the weight of both losses, I see nothing but the dirt before me. It is an enormous effort simply to put one plodding foot in front of the other. I walked this way once: What kind of malevolent God would ask me to walk it again?

Not only would I drag myself to the burial grounds; I would endure the ritual there and the meal afterwards in a state of leaden numbness. And then (I do not want to think this far, but I force myself to imagine)—then, the sympathetic crowd clustering around me would vanish. I would become nameless and faceless to those who had been my neighbors for over twenty years.

My script was rigidly written and I could not change a line. I would take to the streets, begging. I who had always loved my home, who had cooked more meals than I could count, would rely on the scraps of strangers. Once intimately connected, I would drift like refuse blown by the wind. I would haunt the outskirts of town, grateful for a tree's shade, or a random roof in a storm. The flowers I had nurtured would turn to straw. I would become an embarrassment to the noisy surge of ordinary life, a shadowy reminder of death, best kept at a distance.

Perhaps I could cling to a few dear, familiar things (my stomach wrenches at the image of the pitiful knapsack), but the people I had loved, the faces I had met each morning were gone, utterly gone. As anxiously as I had once waited for my son to come home, I would now, with the same intensity, await my death. That desperate vigil would become my only purpose in living.

Thinking of my husband and son, it seems so recently that we all ate together, happy, munching on the bread I had baked, the fruit from my garden. We took such pride in our dates and figs, the first downy apricots. We'd gather around the table with joking and sometimes, music. It hurts too much to remember. Some animal keening sound escapes me. From a place low in my stomach spirals a wail that captures the anguish of an abandoned child.

"Do not weep." The words startle me; all I can think is "What else have I done wrong? Have I lost even the right to cry? Must I justify my tears?" In my exhaustion, I struggle to remember this face. Tears blur my vision as I reach to recall. Who is the stranger who has stopped the procession? Why does he intrude on my private grief?

Before I can intervene, his hand brushes the litter. Even now, my instinct is to protect my son; I reach out as if to save him from another blow. I bump into the stretcher bearers; they too have halted in surprise. When the man told my son to rise, I knew he was delusional. Poor soul, probably ruined by grief too, his ties to reality cut in one savage slice.

Once before, I had given birth. I did not dream it could happen again. In a twenty-year compression of time, the bluish skin tones color with oxygen; the baby's first cry turns into my son's word. Still wet, the infant squirms; still wrapped, the lifeless corpse sits up. I had received two massive blows; I had witnessed two magnificent miracles.

MIRIAM TODAY

Jesus halted the funeral procession and interrupted a process that seemed to grind along inexorably. In his day, people assumed that a woman without a husband or son had become a nothing. With her only identity obliterated, she would be treated like trash. "Stop it," his gesture says. It is not in the

Creator's plan that any precious human being be stripped of her dignity, negated, ignored, driven from the warmth of the community. The widow has intrinsic worth, regardless of whether her husband and son live.

In *Not Counting Women and Children*, Megan McKenna points out that by touching the bier, the place of contamination, Jesus freely places himself with the ostracized Miriam. He resists not only death, but the injustice of a system that casts aside the living.[1]

While we may delude ourselves that such cruelty was practiced only in primitive societies, modern examples abound. While they may not be pretty, they are convincing evidence that Miriam lives on, in a thousand faces and names, with a variety of ethnic backgrounds and sexual orientations. Still she is pushed beyond the pale.

Stories from abroad and at home offer abundant evidence of women being marginalized and victimized. In *Possessing the Secret of Joy*, Alice Walker cites estimates that from ninety to one hundred million women and girls living in African, Far Eastern, and Middle Eastern countries have been genitally mutilated.[2] In parts of the Middle East and North Africa, up to 90 per cent of two- to twelve-year-old girls undergo clitorectomies to make them less sexual, more "faithful" to their husbands.[3]

In *Women in the Church I*, Madonna Kolbenschlag describes a photo of an Indian woman with two babies. The robust boy squirms vigorously. His twin sister looks emaciated and listless because her only nourishment is what's left over after the sturdy boy nurses. Hollow-eyed, she no longer even tries for attention. Kolbenschlag concludes, "I don't think I have ever seen a more graphic picture of the situation of women throughout our civilization."[4] In some parts of India, a girl is forty times less likely than her brother to be taken to a clinic.

In Papua, New Guinea, a teacher noticed how awkwardy the girls approached the chalkboard. As they wrote, they bent their knees and maintained a stooped posture. When the teacher asked why, they explained that they must always keep their heads lower than those of the boys.

An Ethiopian man sauntered along a road, twirling a stick. Behind him plodded a donkey and a woman with two children. Both the donkey and the woman were bent beneath huge loads of hay. Hers, however, was heavier; she served as a beast of burden. A United Nations report stated that women do two-thirds of the world's unpaid work and 51 per cent of the paid work, but receive only 10 per cent of the wages and hold 1 per cent of the property.

In this country, the statistics on domestic violence point to a dirty secret committed behind closed doors. Every fifteen seconds, according to the Colorado Domestic Violence Coalition, a woman in the United States is attacked by a man she loves. At least 2 million women are severely assaulted by their male partners annually; at least fourteen hundred women a year die as a result of domestic violence.

Maya Angelou records in the poem "Our Grandmothers" a string of taunts hurled against her foremothers—taunts which persist today in racist attitudes towards women of color:

> nigger, nigger bitch, heifer,
> mammy, property, creature, ape, baboon,
> whore, hot tail, thing, it.[5]

The abandonment Miriam experienced at Naim is still felt by contemporary women: "Women in the church, especially single 'older' women, are a forgotten entity, and pastors do not know how to respond to their needs. I have experienced this for twenty-eight years as a widow in a Lutheran congregation," said a woman interviewed for *Defecting in Place: Women Claiming Responsibility for Their Own Spiritual Lives* by Miriam Therese Winter and her co-authors.[6] Another, consulted for the study, confided, "I don't remember anyone who actually asked for my opinion."[7]

The accumulated evidence of oppression and isolation is convincing. Yet just as heartening is unflinching defiance and resistance in the face of repeated defeat. Women have a long, noble history of acting as Jesus did at Naim. For instance, four women in Botswana, learning about women's liberation, deliberately sat on a wall. When their teacher asked them why, they explained that until then, they had always sat on the ground. Their shift in position may have been incomprehensible to a North American, but was a gigantic leap forward for them.

Similarly, Peruvian women visited by Madonna Kolbenschlag banded together to solve the problem of wife beating. The men would come home drunk on the weekends and beat them up, so they scraped together enough money to buy whistles. The oldest child in each family was designated to run into the street and blow the whistle when the man began the violence. The women had made a pact: when they heard the whistle, they would all rush outside with their pots and pans and shame the abuser with their din. Their success convinced them that they could imagine and effect change.[8]

When Jesus raised Miriam's son, he gave her back her life. As Megan McKenna points out, he restored "her future, her meaning, her possibility for a life with dignity. . . . He has saved two lives."[9]

In the same way, literature written by women of color contains a lifesaving message. Author Toni Cade Bambara calls her stories of renewal and transformation "sheer holy boldness." She describes her work:

> Stories are important. They keep us alive. In the ships, in the camps, in the quarters, fields, prisons, on the road, on the run, underground, under siege, in the throes, on the verge—the storyteller snatches us back from the edge to hear the next chapter. In which we are the subjects. We, the hero of the tales. Our lives preserved . . . . Passing it along in the relay. That is what I work to do: to produce stories that save our lives."[10]

The son snatched from the bier; the mother's life restored. The story yanking us from the abyss; the relay that connects and sustains. Women who struggle to birth the future act as agents of change unprecedented in human history.

Paradoxically, as they have their consciousnesses raised by their daughters, they also enrich what they will hand on to their children. Perhaps their position is best summarized by a woman quoted in Sara Ruddick's *Maternal Thinking: Toward a Politics of Peace*. When asked by her daughter why she worked so hard for social justice, a young mother replied, "If, in the end, we lose, I will look at you, straight at you, and say I tried."[11]

FOR REFLECTION OR DISCUSSION

1. Recall a time in the past when you felt sure something was dead: a relationship, a project, a goal, your health, or that of a beloved person. If it was in some way restored to life, summon that memory. What was your immediate reaction? Do you still have feelings of surprise and wonder at this restoration? Taste those emotions again, knowing your solidarity with Miriam.

2. After her son was brought back to life, how might Miriam feel towards him? Consider the people you love: What would the loss of them mean? Their restoration? What responsibilities does resurrected life bring—to them as well as to us?

3. Jesus came that we might have life and is outraged when that life is denied. Where do you find evidence of death or decay? Identify the bier in your life: Is it the pollution of the seas? The destruction of the ozone layer? The feminization of poverty? Or something more personal: A cancer in your marriage? Your family? Your neighborhood? Your church? Your office? Your city or nation?

Visualize Jesus touching the place you have identified and taking on your anguish. Hear him saying, "Do not weep." Know that his heart is filled with pity and compassion. What does he see on this bier that no one else can see? What balm does he bring? What do you say to him?

Are some things or relationships better left dead? Visualize Jesus helping you to reverently, gently bless and bury these.

4. Megan McKenna calls miracles manifestations of God's presence among us, trying to snag our attention. The miracles in your life may not be as dramatic as a death-to-life reversal. Yet through daily marvels, God calls, "Do I have your attention yet?" Choose one day of the past week. Identify the minor miracles in it.

5. A question once put from an audience to Megan McKenna challenges us, too. "Have you ever brought someone back from the dead?" Don't cheat and jump ahead to her answer. Instead, use the space below to consider your own response. Before you answer too modestly, remember that Jesus did not change an entire system. In this incident, he affected the lives of two individuals. How have you restored hope, kindled excitement, reassured another person who felt depressed, anxious or guilty? How have you called for accountability, or challenged an evil?

After writing, discussing or thinking about your own reply, consider how McKenna answered the question:

Yes. Every time I bring hope into a situation, every time I bring joy that shatters despair, every time I forgive others and give them back dignity and the possibility of a future with me and others in the community, every time I listen to others and affirm them and their life, every time I speak the truth in public, every time I confront injustice—yes—I bring people back from the dead.[12]

6. The section "Miriam Today" details injustices against women. What was your response to these? What area of injustice most concerns you? Poverty? Ageism? Abuse against women or children? Prejudice against the divorced or gay/lesbian people? Discrimination against ethnic minorities or physically challenged people? Bias against the mentally ill?

   After identifying your area of concern, take inventory of the ways you have already worked against the injustice. Which example of women's actions for justice touched you most? Name one act of creative disobedience or one step toward justice you will take in the future.

10

The Parable of the Missing Mother

(LUKE 15:11–32)

It didn't have to happen that way. We could have sat down and talked it over. But my husband is a hothead, and my sons—one fumes; one sulks. The tension between them had been building, probably since Nathan grew taller than Philip. Something shifted in their relationship when my older son felt threatened. Maybe he worried that Nathan would no longer look up to him, now that he had an inch or two on him in height.

But he wasn't too skilled at reading between the lines. Philip couldn't see that Nathan still copied every gesture, walked with a similar stride, even tried to comb his unruly hair in the same style. It was poignant, how Nathan counted on Philip for approval, the old habit rooted in boyhood. When it wasn't forthcoming (Philip stingy with praise), Nathan would act unthinkingly, and take a risk he'd later lament. Claiming his share of the inheritance was the ultimate insult to Philip, as though in one bold stroke he could reverse the birth order! My husband capitulated, as if to tell Nathan, "I'll pay anything to get you out of here and restore the peace."

I will always regret not being home the weekend of the explosion. I returned from my sister's to find an eerie quiet in the house, and Nathan's empty room. "What have you done?" I accused the men who looked guilty. They were quick to list the charges against Nathan. It had escalated beyond the usual skirmishes, perhaps because I wasn't there to settle it with a little humor, some time apart, a good dinner. They had apparently rushed for huge weapons, battle cries, the whole cosmic scale for a lousy domestic argument.

By the second week, the thrill of the combat had worn off. They were no longer boasting how they'd gotten the better of him, and were starting to worry beneath the cool camouflage of unconcern. Nathan's absence was gnawing away at me; I longed for his quick tongue, the flashing fall of his laughter. He was young and naive; he'd never traveled alone. Was he safe? Had he been mugged along the road? How long would his money last? The questions prodded me awake in the middle of the night, as my husband snored beside me.

After a month, I noticed my husband taking long walks down the road, usually at twilight when there was no reason to work there. Did he scan the horizon for a slight movement, then frown in disappointment? Did his head jerk at the sound of each passing cart? Was he starting to miss Nathan as much as I did?

After four months, I went searching. My husband seemed sunk in a stupor; Philip was sullen and depressed. If that boy was ever to be found and brought home, it was up to me. I spoke with one of the servants, an older woman I could trust, planning the celebration that should take place if Nathan returned while I was gone. She had a detailed list: chilled wine, fatted calf, music. I entrusted her with a ring that had been my father's and soft leather sandals, Nathan's size, that I'd found at the market and saved for a special event. Even if Philip and my husband stewed, I made sure that Nathan would have a proper welcome. Above all, I warned the servant to notify me and gave her an outline of my travel plans.

That was the easy part. I knew that any true celebration required more than party favors. So I gulped deeply and drew on my bottom-line confidence that no matter how messy things look, it can all come together in the end. I began to talk with my husband, knowing that genuine welcome must begin in the heart. If we did not prepare a place for Nathan, we did not deserve to have him back.

It emerged in our talks that my husband recognized his own impetuosity in our younger son. They both had the nature of a spring storm: intense and fierce. They would hurl furious words, then all was calm. Except this time. No one had intervened; no one had suggested a time to cool off. My husband felt terrible about the damage done, and grieved that the loss was permanent. Our affable airhead, our child bursting with dreams and ambition was gone, and it was at least partly his father's fault.

It took a lot of talking, and he needed time to sit with his grief. But I think the incident made a deep impression. We agreed that if Nathan ever did come home, we would not take him for granted again. We would love him for lightning flash and thunderbolt; then we would cradle him securely when the storm was spent.

My servant was true to her word and followed every last direction. By the time they found me, exhausted with the futile search, the wine had gone flat and the leftovers of fatted calf had congealed. No matter—both my boys were safe. I slept with a deep security I hadn't had in months. As I drifted off that first night home, I reviewed the story the servant had told me.

According to her, the first sight of that unbathed boy galvanized his father. He ran down the road with the energy of his youth (and was probably panting by the time he reached Nathan). The servants heard the pounding steps and shouting, so they rushed to see what was happening. Typical of my husband's style: He drowned the boy's apology in his huge embrace. I knew the man's extra-large size; I've sewn his shirts. So I also knew that Nathan had been enveloped in enormous arms, right there on the dusty road.

When my husband called with exuberance for the ring and sandals, of course they were ready and waiting. (He probably thinks all household details happen so spontaneously!) As the serving woman brought the gold and leather, she heard my husband bellow, "This son of mine was dead and has come back to life; he was lost and is found." Ah, the men of my family do love drama!

Of course tomorrow the euphoria will wear off and I'll have to deal with Philip. He's still filled with the poison of resentment and I'll need to find out what's really causing his anger. But I don't know if I can top what my husband told him. The servant reported that he said, "You are with me always and all I have is yours." If that doesn't reassure the boy, I don't know what will. The words have been for me a lovely pillow, the cornerstone of our house, the surety of my husband's good heart.

FOR DISCUSSION OR REFLECTION

1. This version of the parable of the prodigal son responds to Erik Erickson's puzzlement many years ago over a father who loved like a mother. He asked, "Was there no mother, either dead or alive? And if alive, was she not called to say hello, too?" His unanswered question was repeated by the *Women's Bible Commentary*, which gave this chapter its title.[1]

    • How does the shift in perspective alter the parable for you?

    • Do you find the changes distracting, or do they open new windows? Explore your response.

- If you were to rewrite the parable, making shifts in gender and viewpoint, how would you change it? (Telling it with mother and daughters is also an interesting exercise.)

- Regardless of adaptations, what clear message about the nature of God still emerges from the parable?

- Jesus' original audience was the scribes and Pharisees. What group of people, or what part of yourself do you think most needs this message today?

2. The appeal of the parable is its roots in the hassles of family life. Jesus knew that no family was as relentlessly trouble-free, smiling, and sanitized as contemporary advertising and television sometimes tries to make families seem. Someone is usually sulking while someone else is chortling; one daughter laments the effects of overplucked eyebrows, while the other daughter rehearses her lines for the school play. At our kitchen tables, failure and fulfillment sit close enough to pass the potatoes.

   As Thomas Moore points out in *Care of the Soul*, the name of our first father "Adam" means red earth. "Our own families recapitulate this mythic origin of our humanity by being close to the earth, ordinary, a veritable weed patch of human foibles." If we fail to understand our roots in the oily slime, we sentimentalize what the family *should* be and overlook what it is: "a sometimes comforting, sometimes devastating house of life and memory."[2]

   The purest, most incandescent water lilies spring from the muck. Even from families that seem chaotic and dysfunctional, people learn valuable lessons and draw essential security. Perhaps we fully appreciate our families only when we are willing to start where they are, not where we think they should be.

What are the two or three most important happenings that have occured in the complexity of your family life—either your family of origin, your nuclear family, or the people you count as family? Turn these experiences into a teaching, as Jesus did, about the beauty or bounty of God.

Here is an example, a spin on this parable. A policewoman revealed to her mother that she was a lesbian. Her mother was surprised, but accepting. Then the policewoman told her sister, who was outraged. The sister fumed at everyone in sight, but especially at the mother. "How long have you known?" she sputtered. "How could you have put up with it?"

Calmly the mother replied. "I have always loved her, just as she is. So I guess I have always loved her lesbian nature too." What echoes of the prodigal father do you catch in this mother's reply?

3. The unresolved question of the original parable and of this version still hangs over the older son. We never know if he joined the joy. But perhaps less important than "Did he convert?" is the question, "Will we?" Many writers have pointed out that most women still seem locked in the "good kid" syndrome. When the older son complains that he's never had a party with his friends, and now this spoiled upstart who squandered his inheritance gets royal treatment, we nod in sympathy.

It's enough to trigger the litany: "All these years I've plugged away, turning down the party invitations to do the work, keeping my nose clean and my house disinfected, skirting temptation, nobly eating the leftovers no one wants, avoiding risk. I don't do it for the fun of it, no ma'am, nor the pay, nor the pathetically inadequate thanks. Then the crew that cuts out early to splurge on beer and pizza gets rewarded! Sacrificially, I flick off the

TV to study the scripture, and some parable tells me I'm mean-spirited and stingy. Harrumph!" Do we secretly envy those who jump ship, ignore obligations, turn down the good-cause commmittee, and never seem to pay the price for breaking the rules and chucking the niceties?

Where within us does the younger sibling still wink mischievously, still struggle to break free, still long to blow the inheritance, and have a walloping good time with champagne, filet mignon, a new dress with *matching* accessories—the whole works? Identify those yearnings; have a chat with your "younger sibling" self, in which you do not condemn, but seek to understand.

If it is helpful, pull up two chairs and continue the conversation, now including the mature, resentful self. Sit in one chair to be the older sibling and in the other to be the younger sibling. Shift chairs when you switch voices. In what ways does this exercise help to reconcile the different sides of yourself?

4. Repeat the father's words to Philip, substituting your own name, "_____ you are with me always and all I have is yours." Let the assurance lead into prayer. Or use the words to bless another person, substituting that person's name and embracing her or him with the father's warmth.

5. Both older and younger sons resemble their parents. In "coming out" (the same verb is used for both boys) to them, the father may recognize some of his own traits in the brothers. Which of your own traits (including the flaws) do you recognize in your offspring, or in other people? Which of your parents' qualities do you see in yourself?

II

Rebecca,

Mother of the Man Born Blind

(JOHN 9)

My husband did the talking. It's pretty much a man's business, interrogation. Women don't count as legal witnesses—what a relief! I was so excited that my son could see, I couldn't understand how anyone could twist a miracle into a matter of placing blame. I probably would have said, "Of course it's my son, and he was born blind, and isn't it splendid that now he can see?" I might have grabbed the arm of the fusty Pharisee in my delight.

But he didn't have my memories: the little boy's jutting chin, leading him on sheer instinct because he lacked the sight of other children . . . his hands always seeking, waving before him, like tendrils, frail and thin, his sensors . . . other children jeering at him as he bumbled into doors and trees . . . his collapse into bed at night when the whole futile attempt to keep up became too much, even for his plucky spirit . . . his sarcasm developing in adolescence, painfully like my own, the only weapon of the unarmed person.

One day his wit served him well. He'd met a long series of bullies, so he recognized the Sanhedrin and knew how to stand up to them. They thought him stupid because his blindness reduced him to beggary. I could have cheered his rapier tongue: flashing like swordplay, the feints and thrusts practiced in his darkened days and shadowy nights. When they probed for information about his healer, he asked slyly, "Do you want to become his disciples too?"

How he slashed through their deceptions and uncovered the holes in their arguments! How deftly he punctured their smug assumptions and poked the bubble of their entrenched ideas! Bravo, my boy! After years of torment, you had your moment. You emerged squinting from darkness, and stood in a marvelous light.

Stubbornly, he stuck to the truth in his story, so they couldn't budge him. "He can speak for himself," his father had said. Such hard-won understanding squeezed into five words! Over and over, I had to learn that lesson, suppressing my instinct to protect him, stifling pity, saying no to him as directly as I would to any sighted child, pushing him to independence. And the miracle was, he *could* speak for himself: eloquent and bold, even when put through a grilling that would have intimidated trained orators.

Of course, there's more to the story than what got recorded. I still remember, after the crowds went away and we were no longer the day's distraction, his delight in what he'd suddenly seen: the veins in leaves, the low purple hills, blue shadows, beetles, feathers, water flowing from a pitcher. All the things I'd seen a hundred times gleamed, new-minted, for him. In his just-opened eyes, everything took on the sheen of spring. I'll always remember the awe as he told me, "Finally I can see your face!"

That brought tears to *my* eyes, but there was more. Since the day he was born, I'd wondered. The rabbis taught that God created everything, and God is just. If God could create such an affliction, there must be a reason. I knew that the baby, smelling sweet from his bath, had not sinned. I could not escape the logic: then the sin must be in me. The cruel words of the religious leaders (and they should know) only confirmed the condemnation I'd carried in my heart: "You were born totally in sin" (John 9:34).

Over and over, I mined the past, trying to remember. What had I done to submerge an innocent child in an endless night? How had I caused the light to die in his eyes? Oh, I'd done plenty of things wrong: that wasn't what puzzled me. It was more a question of which sin? How I detested the evil in me that could spread like a stain over him. It was worse because it was unknown: a mysterious monster with long claws, ripping everything most precious to me. And somehow I had created the monster.

It gnawed at me even as the cure unfolded. My son's experience so tightly knit with mine, I started to wonder: why had I taught *him* to be outspoken, then let my husband speak for me? Of course it was custom; no woman ever spoke for herself. My husband was desperately trying to protect our spot in the synagogue. If we were thrown out, we couldn't endure it! After years of hearing the undertones, the nasty whispers circulating about our sin, how could we toss aside what little security we had seized? Even as he played dumb, I could hear the rumor mills cranking up again, the cracks shattering our comfort zone.

Here's the strange thing: I was starting not to care. Even as my son blinked, as his watery eyes dilated and focused, I was starting to see through what I'd held most sacred. Had I been blinded by the beauty of our ritual, lulled by our chanted song? I had always worshiped in the tradition of my parents and grandparents, but was it partly sham? Could a broader vision include my son and all the others banished from the temple's inner courts, the pitiful fringe begging outside?

I had never known that the light in someone's eyes could have such force. The sudden sparkle in my son's wide gaze dealt a death blow to the bestial guilt I carried within. My son's vision restored my own.

He freed me from caring what other people think, from placating the synagogue crowd. It's as if he said, "Ah, there's so much more to see!" His talk spilled over with the wonders he'd viewed, but he kept coming back to one face.

This Jesus had not, like the arrogant authorities, pre-emptorily summoned him. Jesus had sought him out. My son cherished their moment together: I could tell by all the details in his story and the excitement in his voice. "I was honest with him. I asked him, 'Who *is* this Son of Man?' I'm not afraid of stupid questions; I've asked them all my life. I thought it was just one more thing everyone else took for granted, but I'd never seen. He didn't jeer at me like everyone else does. He said, 'You have seen him.' And all of a sudden, I knew why my sight was restored. Even if I plummeted back into blackness, I'd had this recognition. I'd looked into his face. That memory burns so bright, I could almost live with blindness again."

He told me then, my proud child with the craggy profile, who had never stooped to anyone, who had clung to his last shred of dignity, how he had bowed in worship before Jesus. My hero had laid his sword at the teacher's feet; he had no need of it now.

I saw the world through his eyes then, newly washed as from rain, glinting in the sun, almost too beautiful to bear. I too had fresh vision. Guilt had slipped off my shoulders just as scales had fallen from his eyes. I walked as if a cave once dark within me were flooded with all the world's light.

REBECCA TODAY

The story of Rebecca's son is woven with many colors and rich ambiguity. A lively interplay of themes runs throughout: light and shadow, blindness and sight, silence and voice, healing and condemnation. It begins as Jesus is walking along, and is filled with movement. The question that precipitates the whole miracle sounds as callous as interns in a hospital oncology ward cruelly speculating on who sinned: the patients or their parents?

Yet the disciples are simply people of their times. Because the ancient Hebrews believed that illness must be the result of sin, they had almost no science of medicine and no doctors, compared with their contemporaries in Greece, who had fairly advanced knowledge of anatomy and relatively sophisticated forms of treatment.

With admirable swiftness, Jesus pivots from the narrow view and the academic exercise to the direct—and, in this case, dirty—work of healing the individual. It is as if he deliberately chooses the most basic elements—spit and mud—to show his preference for action over theory.

Ironically, the cure causes a flurry of theorizing. It threatens authorities whose positions are entrenched and who refuse to let facts interfere with assumptions. The Pharisees would never dirty their robes or their rules with spittle, dirt, or (God forbid) humanity! Jesus opens a whole new way of seeing.

At first, that comes as a threat to Rebecca, who remains silent. But we can't help wondering if she had second thoughts. We can't suppress our suspicion that if the authorities had come back a second time, the maternal parent might have told a different story . . .

Women today confront the same ambiguity about religious authority that may have troubled Rebecca. On one hand, we have been taught to respect that voice. On the other, we see how it can damage us, piling on a burden of guilt. One side of us rejects authority, asserting, "Don't let anyone ever tell you you are deformed, dysfunctional, seductive, sinful. You are made in God's own image." Another voice whispers, "Maybe they're right."

Defecting in Place: Women Claiming Responsibility for Their Own Spiritual Lives by Miriam Therese Winter and others cites contemporary examples of this dilemma from women of all religious traditions. A fifty-year old finds that her need to

outgrow father figures and discover her own inner authority
leads her outside the Catholic Church. A Hispanic woman
expresses her frustration that while her people are asked for
endless volunteer hours, church administrators usually hire
an Anglo for a paid position. A mother weighs her responsibility to belong to a faith community for her children's sake
against her own abhorrence for the institution. Another
woman agonizes over religious leaders' obsession with control, "so contrary to the spirit of Christianity as I understand
it that I feel deeply betrayed."[1] Many women turn in disgust
from authoritarian structures, male-dominated rites, and
exclusive language to find their own way. Perhaps Rebecca
could guide their quests.

FOR REFLECTION OR DISCUSSION

1. While despair with church leadership may be legitimate,
    we know that we can't blame the authorities for our own
    blind spots. Where have we failed to see through a bel-
    ligerant adult or arrogant employer to a frightened
    child? How often do we accept face value, refusing to
    look deeper? In what areas of our lives is it easier, sim-
    pler, faster to put on the blinders, avoiding the direct
    and painful look? When do we, due to frenzied sched-
    ules and hurried days, overlook the small beauties and
    fragile wonders of creation? Where do we need Jesus to
    open our eyes?

2. David Brower, former executive director of the Sierra
    Club, one of the nation's leading environmentalists and
    author of seven books, attributes much of his energy
    and insight to the boyhood experience of becoming the
    eyes for his mother. Although she went blind while still
    in her early forties, she liked to be outdoors. So, at the
    age of seven, he became her guide.
        He describes a hike to Grizzly Peak, 1,759 feet high.
    "It was a joyful thing, that first big walk. It was my job

to tell my mother where to put her feet in the rough places, and which one, right or left, but there was no great worry. . . . At the top, I described the vista for her: the hills; the galaxy of flowers; the few new houses; a red-tailed hawk floating on the wind, looking for field mice; the fog coming over San Francisco Bay; the glimpse of the open sea through the Golden Gate." Seeing and describing "all that wild beauty" for his mother, he became intent on preserving it.[2]

What kind of sight did Rebecca give her blind son? How did he, in turn, later give her new sight? Who has helped you see things in a new or different light? How?

Sometimes seeing is a question of adjusting our lenses. The story is told of three people asked about their work. One said, "I chisel stone." Another said, "I'm supporting my family." A third said, "I am building the great cathedral of Chartres!" All three did the exact same work: but what a difference in perspective!

Shift the metaphor to your own life, where all three viewpoints may come into play. Sometimes we say, "I'm a computer operator;" at other times, "I'm making $15.20 an hour to pay the orthodontist and the rent." At our peak moments we say, "I am building the reign of God." What accounts for the differences in description?

3. Here are three quotes about sight or vision. Choose the one that resonates for you and spend some time this week reflecting on it.

    •   "The people who sat in darkness have seen a great light, and for those who sat in the region and shadow of death, light has dawned."—Matt. 4:16

    •   "More precious was the light in your eyes than all the roses in the world."[3]—Edna St. Vincent Millay

    •   "Sick people and old people are perfectly aware that nothing much matters but love and bread and little

glass beads. It makes no difference whether the
beads come from Tiffany's or Woolworth's as long as
they catch the sun."[4]—Marshall Sprague

4. Rebecca's story raises questions about religious authority.
    Some women today live in two churches, caught in a love–
    hate relationship. Others seek alternate forms of prayer
    and spiritual nurture, outside of institutional structures.

    How do you handle this tension, discerning what to
    honor in your religious tradition, and what may be
    harmful? Or, what in your tradition is life-giving? What
    is death-dealing?

5. Think about the burden of guilt you may carry from the
    past. Perhaps the worst kind of evil is the one that has
    affected others—innocent children, friends, spouses, or
    relatives. When we bear the responsibility for harm
    done to them, it can crush us. For a few moments, feel
    that weight, slumping your shoulders, dragging down
    your center of gravity. Walk around a room for a few
    minutes beneath that burden.

    Then imagine Jesus freeing you from that guilt.
    Hear in your heart the words of Jesus which onlookers
    reported to Rebecca: "Neither he nor his parents
    sinned." Faith teaches that those words are also
    addressed to us. Feel their echo deep inside. How does
    that message of liberation make you feel? Walk around a
    room now showing in your movement the difference six
    words can make in a person's attitude. Express in your
    walk the words of dancer Sandra Riviera, about her
    work with children: "I try to get kids to fill their bodies
    with light, to internalize light."[5]

    In his gratitude to Jesus, the formerly blind man
    said little, ("Lord, I believe"), but his gesture expressed
    it all: he bowed in worship. Through reverent gesture,
    speak your gratitude to Jesus.

12

Salome:

Blunder and Blessing

(MATT. 20:20–29)

How cruel, that wherever the gospel is preached, I should be remembered for my mistake. I'm notorious for one blunder; I'll always be the ultimate pushy mother. No one pays attention to the rest of my story, but then quiet, steady service never makes headlines. By now I've eluded the definitions of other people; I'll tell my own tale.

The pressures had been building like gnats buzzing close to my face. "What about jobs for those boys?" my mother whined. "They're at an age when all their friends have settled down," my best friend murmured. Zebedee was more direct: "We have a fleet to maintain! All my life, I've worked hard to build this fishing business! Are they going to abandon it? How can you stand by silent, watching our ruin? Discipline them!"

Surreptitiously, I watched James and John. I could not be objective about my handsome sons, their skin shining wet from the lake, their muscles bulging as they hauled in the nets. Once, they would have shouted in glee over a big catch. But now there was something more to their lives than fishing, some mystery stirring beneath the surface of the waters.

They seemed so happy around Jesus; in his presence, they drew closer to each other than ever before. If it is possible, they had more verve; they churned with robust energy. James and John had found a certain rightness, as though they had finally discovered whatever they searched for in their turbulent adolescence. They relaxed and laughed as they had in childhood. They didn't worry about jobs or incomes; they had all the security they needed in him. They had come into still waters; I hated to rock the boat.

But I was torn: how could I tune out the voices of my husband, my elders? For years I had been schooled to respect their wisdom. Surely my mother knew how to raise boys; she kept underlining my failure. Was it too late to correct my shameful wrong? Could I steer them toward respectability again? If these boys were ever to shape up, it was my responsibility. Zebedee would shout angrily at them; they would avoid him; stalemate again. I kept pushing myself: At the very least, I would try.

Maybe I could find some middle ground, I told myself. Could they stay close to Jesus *and* earn a living? Why did happiness exclude civic responsibility? Everyone I knew had a home, security: how could my boys be cheated of their birthright? Did Jesus demand something unnatural of them?

Then one day, I got an inspiration. Jesus had uncanny power. What's more, he clearly loved my boys; why couldn't he assure their success? They'd left decent jobs to follow him: didn't he owe something in return? Propelled by this burst of insight, I ran, falling over myself, to Jesus.

In later years, I've wished I'd taken more time to weigh the idea, but then it seemed like the perfect answer. I even embellished it: matched thrones on either side! I could imagine my boys with golden crowns, their glory stifling doubt. At the sight of their high status in the kingdom, critics would fall silent, embarrassed by their own skepticism.

Beneath the fantasy, I grasped a kernel of truth: They would still be close to Jesus. They would be deeply fulfilled and I would die happy. How could I *not* engineer a solution that would satisfy everyone? Filled with self-congratulation, I almost forgot my manners. Then I remembered: a last-minute, quick-save bow to Jesus, who was, after all, crucial to the plan.

I saw his face before I heard his reply. If only words hung in the air like balls that could be caught, I would have retrieved my request then. I could have backtracked with a quick apology. But I was not so lucky.

Actually, the response fell less sharply than I anticipated. I had heard him tear into the Pharisees; I knew the wrath he poured on the scribes. But he dealt gently with a mother, maybe knowing how we sometimes swallowed common sense when a child's need beckoned. He tried to excuse my ignorance, soften his answer by saying I didn't know what I asked. My fond hopes for James and John trembled in the air between us; he would not recklessly destroy a dream.

Nor would he dilute his own convictions. When he offered them his cup, I knew instinctively that he wasn't distilling some sweet and heady wine. He meant an acid bath of pain. I wanted to warn the boys, muzzle them and spirit them out of there before they answered. I dreaded their thoughtless generosity. "We can drink it," they trumpeted, and I bit my lip. If I hadn't already said too much, I would have intervened again: "Jesus, don't you see they're young and naive? It's not fair to ask them this! All without payment?"

But by then he had pivoted from my bumbling question, in his typical style of seizing the teaching moment. What a paradox that my fumbling should be the springboard for his soaring words, "Anyone who wants to be first among you must be your slave." So that's it, I thought. Now I understand. It clicked like a lid fitting tight on a box.

The success I had envisioned wore the tired sameness of solutions everyone had tried, but no one had found fulfilling.

What I really wanted for my sons was larger than a throne, more lasting than a gold crown. How could I have forgotten the words singing through my own tradition: "Why spend money on what is not bread, your wages on what fails to satisfy?" When Jesus said, "This is not to happen among you," he was echoing Isaiah. As he shut a door, he blew the ceiling open.

As it turned out, they got what I asked for, in ways I never anticipated. In one sense I was right: they couldn't be happy away from him. John sat beside Jesus at the Last Supper; James was the first Apostle to die, martyred by Herod Agrippa. Their intimacy with Jesus overflowed like some nurturing rain on our household churches.

How do I know? Funny you should ask. After my terrible gaffe, I took to heart the words once addressed to Andrew and Peter. Deep into the cesspool of regret and embarrassment, Jesus' voice penetrated like light. "Come and see," he'd said, and the boys reported the invitation. The casual words tossed to young men had become my lifeline. I am, I discovered, a lot like my sons. Where else did they get their pluck, their sensitivity, their willingness to follow? We shared the same reckless impulse to abandon everything for Jesus.

"Come and see," he dared people who knew perfectly well he had no home and no way to entertain guests. So naturally, I went. The house where he lived was unimpressive, furnished with a few battered discards, not too imaginative in the decorating department. But then I found "where he was staying," that place inside himself where he touched bedrock. It was as though God's magnificent power, that hurls hailstorms and spews volcanoes, that sears the sky with lightning and electrifies the stallion, were contained in him as in a river's banks.

At the same time, deep currents swirled there. I drank of the tenderness that had tempered his words when he could have condemned me. He brought us bread with maternal concern, the light brush of his hand soothing the scar tissue of the old hurts. I could no more have left than I could have stopped a captivating story in midsentence. Beyond curiosity, I wanted to learn from him how to serve.

I had to finesse a few other obligations, but I handled that rather creatively. Zebedee was annoyed, with the whole family taking off, but I would not cave in again. This time, I explained my decision with a conviction I had lacked when he criticized the boys. After casting futilely, I had sunk my anchor securely. It didn't sound logical to my incredulous mother or cynical husband; all I could tell them was "come and see." I know only that now I am in God; I am a flower turned to sun or a channel to the sea. This is my truth; within it, I stand firm.

It may sound airy, but my certainty lasted through some savage tests. It carried me through the rest of Jesus' life, when I exchanged the sure sleep in the familiar bed for the sound of his voice on waking. It enabled me to leave the tidy routine of my household and rely on the kindness of strangers. It brought me to Calvary, where the tears flowed but I leaned into God's grace. Without a tremor, I could hear words that gave John to another mother, and feel honored that he should take Mary into his care. I realized then that Jesus had forgiven my sons and me; he had completely forgotten the old rebuke. Finally, I came to the tomb with my friends and discovered a second spring, another resurrection, a surge of life that never ends.

SALOME TODAY

Salome's dilemma will sound familiar to anyone who loves a child or another person so much they want to intervene for them, take their blows, nudge them ahead. We of the modern era also live in a society that values achievement and steers its youth into the secure niche of the corporate power structure. Peer pressure is familiar: how often have we worried about a loved one who marches to a different drummer?

Under stress, we do things for another person that we would never do for ourselves. We go out of our way, make the phone call, manipulate the connection and overlook our own discomfort. We wonder vaguely why we would grovel for the sake of another, when we'd detest that impulse on our own behalf. "Self-sacrifice!" comes the clarion call; while a quiet voice questions, "Isn't this a bit *much*?"

Like Salome, we may sense that a part of us is confused, sending up smoke signals of doubt. If we are fortunate, someone like Jesus calls forth the better self. He invites us to step into the part that has clarity: smooth as sand, clean as morning. He gives us the examples of people who are well grounded and leads us, as he did Salome, into the place of tranquility.

Perhaps it is a measure of Salome's surety that she does not berate herself endlessly for her mistake. Sin and grace are companions close enough to dance together; people who are broken and vulnerable are often the most likely candidates for sainthood. Salome moves from the pits to the heights, unafraid of growth and the pain it necessarily entails. She finds that miracles can occur when we leave safety and push to the edge. Like her sons, she finds the only home she needs in the person of Jesus. As conformity to external pressures becomes less important to her, she finds that she receives an unexpected, but ultimately satisfying answer to her request. She fits the description written by Karen Blixen (Isak Dinesen), in a letter from Ngong, Kenya: "And you—you have begun to *live*— which means: to find your joy and your oblivion in the grace of God. Nothing better can befall a human being."[1]

FOR REFLECTION OR DISCUSSION

1. In Matthew's version of this story (20:20–29), Salome pops the question about her sons' advancement. In Mark's version (10:35–40) James and John ask for promotion themselves, causing consternation when the other disciples get wind of their self-serving request.

The incident could have happened either way, but something about the mother's intervention rings true. We nod in empathy: we have all acted quickly and foolishly, then regretted our haste. Is Salome really the archetypal pushy mother, whose descendants shove their offspring into the spotlight? Do we recoil at the thought of the intent mama backstage, on the sidelines, relentlessly coaching, constantly running interference? Or do we tend to give Salome more sympathy than she deserves?

On the other hand, it is perfectly plausible that young men would try to jostle for the top spots. To transpose them into the twentieth century, imagine the Zebedee boys—all flash of polyester and gold chains around the neck, drooling for the perks, the wood-paneled and brass-plated executive suite, the cushioned lifestyle, the corporate jet.

Which version do you prefer? Why?

2. Sometimes the people closest to us often set the harshest limits on our growth. If we change the dance step, it affects their polished routine. They may prefer to remain locked in a robotic two-step rather than experience the doubtful joys of insecurity.

    The dissonance between us only reflects the fact that human relationships on earth are flawed and symphonies remain unfinished. One of several unanswered questions lofting through Salome's story is: What happened to Zebedee?

    Imagine, role-play, or write the dialogue that occurred between Salome and Zebedee when she decided to join her sons and follow Jesus. Then if you wish to extend this into the personal realm, imagine, role-play, or write a dialogue between yourself and someone you love about a decision you have made which threatens change for both of you.

3. While a decision may be made in a moment, its effects last longer. T. S. Eliot could have been describing Salome's conversion when he wrote in "Four Quartets":

> . . . Not the intense moment
> Isolated, with no before and after,
> but a lifetime burning in every moment.[2]

Reflect on patterns in your own life: the momentous decisions, followed by the steady commitment to living them out. What enables you to remain faithful? How do you distinguish between a healthy dedication and a sick self-martyrdom? Where do you find God in that process?

4. Salome got her heart's desire—in a way she never expected. How has that phenomenon occured in your life? How have paths you would never deliberately choose brought you closer to Christ?

Mary Catherine Bateson maintains in *Composing a Life* that we need more fluid ways of improvising now that it is less possible to pursue the same career throughout a lifetime.[3] Surely for Salome, discontinuity represented challenge and growth.

What price did Salome pay for her new way of life? In opting for the temporary shelter of Jesus' followers, what permanent dwelling did she find instead?

What changes in your trajectory have been life-giving? How have you relearned your craft or shifted your role? Or does change frighten you? Do you cling to continuity, no matter how flawed it may be?

5. "Since when are words the only acceptable form of prayer?"[4] Dorothy Day once asked. Her question suggests a preference for the concrete over the abstract, the specific and sensible over the heady and academic. Salome describes her relationship with Christ in terms of

images: the precious liquid cupped in the hands, the plant in sunlight, the channel to the sea.

Other images that may prompt prayer are these:

- God says: "I will draw my breath and thy soul shall come to me as a needle to a magnet."[5]—Mechthild of Magdeburg

- "Our souls are candles of the Lord, lit on the cosmic way."[6] — Rabbi Abraham Heschel

- "God is desperate, forever scraping the bottom of the barrel, looking for idiots to change the world."[7] — Edwina Gateley

Choose the image (your own or another's) that you find most conducive to prayer and let it lead you there.

Or enter prayer through action. Salome was one of the band of women whose service and financial backing supported Jesus' mission. They were the foremothers, preferring the particulars to the theological arguments (not that women haven't also excelled at the theoretical!)

Women's preference for action is clear in Mary's visit to her cousin Elizabeth. Richard Rohr writes, "If I found out I was to be the Mother of God, the first thing I would plan would be a thirty-day retreat or something. . . . I would go inside my head." Yet for Mary, action takes priority. "God can teach me in my taking care of my pregnant cousin, in moving towad the world as it is."[8]

Which of your ordinary actions are most prayer-filled? (These are not restricted to the kitchen, but may occur in the boardroom, operating room, garage, lab, classroom, nursery, factory, studio, shop, courtroom, office, theater, or the infinite number of places where women work out their commitments.) What helps you to appreciate the hidden dimension of prayer in action?

13

Martha's

Splendid Moment

(JOHN 11:1-53)

I don't know what possessed me to say it. But I suspect that my mouth, which had gotten me into trouble my whole life, had for a stunning second become my glory. "I believe that you are the Messiah, the Son of God, the one coming into the world," I affirmed, and I meant every word of it.

What drove me to it was not so much his question as his tone, which seemed to quiver with hope. He had never sounded so tentative before; his voice had not wavered on any of his brave assertions. But now it seemed as if his next step, indeed, all that would follow, hung on my response.

I was hardly at my best then: vulnerable, grieving, enraged, and exhausted. I had stayed with Lazarus throughout his last night, watching for every breath, observing closely as his skin paled. As he weakened, I remembered the times he had firmly protected me. He was always the gentler one, but he'd intervene when I got too rambunctious. His soft-spoken manner calmed the other kids, even though they itched to retaliate for my latest verbal jab or foot-in-mouth remark.

Now he lay too sick to eat, even the favorites I'd fixed. Aching, he clutched miserably at the sheets, my wrists. When I saw the veins bulging in his hands, I sent for Jesus. Mary had been reluctant to bother him, but I overrode her fretting that he might be busy.

"Busy!" I wanted to scream. "Don't you think *I'm* busy, running this household by myself?" Mary is—to put it delicately—the sensitive type. In other words, she'd never check a burning pot or start the laundry she needed in time to get it dry. Once she's absorbed in a story, the house could burn down around her ears and she'd never notice. I admire her flair for the dramatic gesture; I wish I'd thought to anoint Jesus. But I can't resist asking, "So who's paying for the perfume?"

I had once, most indiscreetly, raised that issue with Jesus. It was still a sore spot, the memory of him defending her. Maybe it rubbed me wrong because I recognized in him the way Lazarus had always stuck up for me.

My mind rambles, as it does when I am tired. I was so outraged at Jesus' delay that I spewed pure venom when he arrived. Lazarus's place at our table was empty, the brother I loved had vanished, and Jesus became the target for my fury.

Folks with better social skills might have welcomed him with, "Thanks for trying," or even, "Your friend is dead," but I immediately dumped the guilt trip: "If you had been here, my brother would not have died."

Even though Jesus is used to my outspokenness, the accusation hurt; I could tell by the sadness in his eyes. Still, it didn't paralyze him; maybe he continued our conversation because he could trust me. I'd just proven that I wouldn't mask the truth. I would look him straight in the eye, without a shred of syrupy politeness. One pressing issue hovered in the air between us: Was he avoiding the tragedy, or coming at it from another angle? Why was he questioning my belief in the afterlife?

"I know that God will give you whatever you ask." I bit my tongue and tempered my words, softening each syllable, not blurting out in my usual style. I wanted to shout like a furious child, "Bring Lazarus back!" but for my brother's sake, I tried to adopt Jesus' indirect tone.

Despite my restraint, he still hesitated. It was as if he needed something from me, some mysterious affirmation before he plunged ahead. The roles were reversed: just when I needed to lean on him in grief, he asked for my support!

I summoned everything I could give, maybe to answer that longing in his eyes. Down deep, I still wanted my brother back, but the loss had grown beyond a few people. It was a larger matter now, and I was in deep waters. Even if I had lost Lazarus, I could still encourage Jesus. He was the closest thing I had to another brother; I buoyed him up as if he were my own.

Maybe he had taught me how to give people exactly what they need: he had wept with Mary; he had discussed ideas with me; now it was my turn to answer the question he hated to ask. So few people understood him; all he wanted was one person to show some inkling.

And I did know who he was. From all the meals we'd eaten together, all the walks we'd taken, all the conversations that stretched late into the night emerged his shining holiness. I couldn't explain how I knew; I certainly couldn't tell you what text I'd consulted. But in some quiet, sure place within, I was bedrock certain of his power. So I said it aloud.

I hate to sound arrogant, but Jesus forged into that foul-smelling tomb as if propelled by my words. Had I dispatched him to battle death? I ran after him, just in time to see Lazarus lurch forth. My heart pounding, I unwound the burial cloths as if I unwrapped a splendid gift. Three days before, weeping, I had covered his eyes, his nose, his ears with the same linen. Lazarus's face emerging then was the dearest sight in all the world. He looked rumpled and wrinkled, as if woozy from a nap.

I poured so much attention into Lazarus, still shaky and bewildered, that I barely thanked Jesus, or noticed him leave. But neighbors said he walked purposefully toward Jerusalem, driven as he had been to Lazarus's grave. Did my words still echo in his ears? Had I ignited some fire within him? As I had a hundred times before, I asked myself, "*Now* what have I said?"

MARTHA TODAY

If Martha lived today, she would probably be an executive with IBM or the CEO of General Motors. She had administrative skills and relished intellectual exchange. Jesus' appreciation of her unique gifts shows that we become holy by becoming who we are, not by trying to be someone else.

While other aspects of Martha's story are clearly told in the Gospel, her shining moment gets less coverage. Jesus asks Peter a similar question: "Who do you say that I am?" (Mark 8:29). Peter responds, "You are the Messiah!" but then rebukes Jesus for teaching that his passion is the necessary step to his resurrection. For his obtuseness, Jim Dunning in *Echoing God's Word* christens Peter "one of the first Christians to mouth a doctrine or creed without the foggiest idea of what it means."[1] Jesus responds by calling him Satan.

Martha, on the other hand, gives Jesus precisely what he needs to journey to Jerusalem where his passion and death await. Where Peter challenges, Martha supports. Peter's expression of doubt could be debilitating; Martha's affirmation energizes.

While Martha's style is outspoken, her purpose is similar to much of what we now know about female modes of expression. Mary Belenky and the other authors of *Women's Ways of Knowing* point out:

> The life work of many women focuses on maternal practice, where the main goal is to bring the smallest, least members up into relations of equality. While

> mothers and daughters slip into chairs around the
> kitchen table with ease, only occasionally do fathers
> abdicate their platforms without pressure from below.[2]

Women have often been criticized for a kind of discourse
in which they pose questions more frequently than men, listen for longer stretches and refrain from speaking out.
Deborah Tannen's research on gender-based differences in
linguistics supports those characteristics. She found that
from a young age, men view conversation as a negotiation in
which to gain the upper hand and preserve independence.
Women, on the other hand, focus on maintaining connections and preserving intimacy.[3]

Such qualities are sometimes considered marks of
women's powerlessness and passivity, and are criticized for
being tentative and vacillating. However, this pattern is indis-
pensable to those who are learning to articulate. Just as ther-
apists refrain from speaking in order to draw out the voices of
their patients, so women's restraint encourages the voices of
the hesitant. The ability to ask the right question and wait out
an awkward formulation of the answer may run counter to the
more adversarial male style, but it is crucial. Belenky and her
co-authors conclude: "We argue that women's mode of talk,
rather than being denigrated, should become a model for all
who are interested in promoting human development."[4]

Jesus was not a child and Martha was not mothering him.
But the respect and courtesy that characterize their exchange
teach profoundly about the potential for nurture in human
relationships where support is freely given and attention
carefully paid.

FOR REFLECTION OR DISCUSSION

1. To appreciate Martha, it may help to reflect on times
   when you said the right thing or the wrong thing. Most
   human communication hovers in the grey zones, but
   sometimes a comment is precisely on target—or dismally
   off. How do your own successes or failures in speech

help you to understand Martha? Do you know anyone like Martha, or is there a bit of her in yourself?

2. Martha's act of faith and her distinction as the first to proclaim the Messiah spring from her moment of greatest crisis. Has that paradox been true for you? Why or why not?

3. What about all the Lazaruses who don't get raised? If this story prompts you to grieve some loss, that is natural. The poet Edna St. Vincent Millay wrote about these unraised Lazaruses:

> Down, down, down into the darkness of the grave
> Gently they go, the beautiful, the tender, the kind;
> Quietly they go, the intelligent, the witty, the brave.
> I know. But I do not approve. And I am not resigned.[5]

When have you felt this way? What would you tell Martha about your own losses? What would you like to say to Jesus?

4. Just as the glory of God is revealed in the affirmation of Martha and the raising of Lazarus, so God's life continues to surge forth in human beings. Janie, the heroine of Zora Neale Hurston's novel *Their Eyes Were Watching God* has endured two loveless marriages to abusive husbands. She feels as though the glittering spark God placed in her at the beginning has been squelched by mud. When she finally meets a respectful, loving man, she feels authentic love for the first time. "So her soul crawled out from its hiding place."[6]

   Jesus calls to you as he did to Lazarus and Janie, "Come forth!" What tomb must you leave behind? What propels you to respond to his call? How would you answer this challenge from St. Augustine to his faith community: "Are you no longer hoping? Behold, Christ is alive; and hope is dead in you!"

5. Notice all the names for Jesus that appear in this passage (John 11:1–53): Rabbi, Lord, Messiah, Son of God, the

one coming into the world, Teacher. Linger with the one you like best, or another name for Jesus. Enter into prayer by repeating that name, as often as you wish, at any speed you wish.

6. God comes to us where we live and wants us to be who we are. The parable of the pearl shows that we find the treasure on our own ground. Just as Jesus treated Martha and Mary in the unique ways that meant the most to each of them, so Jesus gives you exactly what you need. Savor the sweetness of those gifts for a few moments in silence, or describe them aloud to a friend.

7. According to the *Women's Bible Commentary*, Martha's dilemma was: "Can I let go of the limits that one places on what is possible in order to embrace the limitless possibilities offered by Jesus?"7 To what extent do you sympathize with this dilemma, or make Martha's quandary your own? Poet Mary Oliver could have been answering that question when she wrote:

> What I want to know, please, is
> what is possible, and what is not.
> If it is not, then I am for it.[8]

Maybe at some times we are able to take this high-hearted, defiant stance, and at other times we need more security. Has there been evidence of such times in your own life? Reflect on and describe them both.

8. When Jesus solicits Martha's declaration, he reveals a deeply human need for affirmation. What does this tell you about your own need for affirmation? About the same need in the people around you? In responding to that need, what do we let go of? What do we embrace? Who has "heard you into speech"? For whom have you acted as Martha did for Jesus? In giving or receiving affirmation, what do we discover about the core of the person?

ANOINTED HOUR

Tenacity drives her past
the sneers and to his side.
As alabaster splinters
fragrance fills the room.
Unleashed torrent of her hair
crests, silken on his feet.
Her fingers massage his scalp
tracing arcs, whorls, spirals.

Her coppery trumpet summons
to the inevitable hour, but
not without caress of balm.
Intimate, the rhythmic motion
reaching to the roots, soothing.
Beneath her hands he is anointed.
She kindles the memory of David's
forehead wet beneath Samuel's horn.

Her scented thumb draws a bead of oil
down his temple, molds contours of care,
marks the tender pattern on his head
(the path before him straight, doomed).
As if she could stay the sentence, or
quell the death threat with her palm.
Her bold act assures him: at least
the ordeal ahead begins in beauty.

14

Deborah:

Serving a Meal, Turning a Corner

(MATT. 26:20–30; JOHN 13:1–16

I'd served a hundred of these dinners, but this one was different. I anticipated the usual friendship meal, the familiar Passover foods, the men gathering intimately around their teacher. Only later in the evening, after plenty of wine, would they notice me, and try to pinch me, or ask to walk me home.

It didn't happen as I expected. For one thing, I lost my job. I had fetched the water basin and towel, and was just rolling up my sleeves to wash the dirty, calloused feet. Not that I minded. I liked the rivulets of water cleansing the ugly scars and bunions, the way people relaxed when I massaged their arches. It took so little to bring so much pleasure. Naturally, I was shocked when the master arose and asked to borrow my bowl.

I was even more stunned by his courtesy. This teacher not only washed feet: He looked into people's eyes and talked with them as he stroked a swollen ankle. Then he *kissed* that unlovely anatomy! I thought I was a pro; people seemed satisfied with my work—until I watched his sure touch. Then I knew I had met my match. Afterwards, I would try to remember how his hands looked, and reach for that care myself.

He handled Peter's protest just as deftly, then he motioned to me. Bewildered, I couldn't understand what he meant, until I found myself eased into a chair, and *my* feet being washed with the respect accorded Claudia, the governor's wife! For those few moments I relished a dignity as foreign to me as the master doing the servant's task.

But maybe it wasn't that strange. Maybe Jesus was reminding me of my heritage. My ancestor Deborah began with a menial task, too: keeper of the tabernacle lamps. But she moved beyond it because she burned with indignation at the affronts to her people. She roused the men from their apathy: even General Barak desperately needed her beside him in battle. After her military victory, she assumed authority over Israel and brought peace to the land. Just then, with my feet gleaming wet, I felt as stout-hearted as she. I whispered to myself her song: "Let those who love you be like the sun when it arises in all its strength!" (Judg. 5:31)

The men's voices hushed as Jesus patted my feet dry. What was he trying to teach them? And would they ever get it?

After that extraordinary pause, the conversation resumed its intensity. Caught up in serving the food, I didn't hear much, but when silence fell over the room, I paid attention. This teacher knew how to grab interest! He gave the traditional prayers for blessing a meal an unheard-of twist, calling the bread his body, the wine his blood. As he breathed the words "remember me" with awful finality, I tingled with cold fear. Did something sinister threaten this man who seemed so kind?

Later, in the kitchen, one of the other serving girls answered my question. She had overheard him say that his betrayer was there with him at the table. So the close circle had harbored enemies! Suddenly I visualized Jesus trying to light a lamp with gloomy monsters rearing up around him, evil winds snuffing the flame . . .

My thoughts were interrupted when he sought me to offer bread and wine. "Don't you know I'm just the maid?" I wanted to ask. "*I* should be doing this for *you!*" I took the food to save him embarrassment, but he had totally disrupted our smoothly oiled routines.

Usually a prophet hands on his mantle; a warrior his sword and shield; a rabbi, the legal code or Torah. But Jesus gave us bread to hold his memory, wine to cup his spirit. What a womanly thing to do!

BREAD AND CUP FOR EACH OTHER: WOMEN MEDITATE ON EUCHARIST

Jesus took bread in his hands. We too are a chosen people, lifted into God's hands. Like the Israelites, we were not chosen because we were the biggest or brightest, but because we were loved. As St. Ignatius Loyola might say, "God has a dream for us."[1] Each miniscule step in our making—the precise knitting in the womb, the parents and schools, the siblings and mentors, the terrain in which we took root, the unique talents—these elements are woven into the person who comes, often unconscious of the complex weave, to Eucharist. But God knows intimately the mysterious mix, recognizes the face, and greets us by name.

A homilist once told the story of Eileen, a nurse who put in a strenuous day. From the time she arose, people called her name: "Eileen, where's my blue suit?" "Eileen, we need you to work pediatrics." "Eileen, set up an IV." "Eileen, could you get me lunch when you go?" "Telephone, Eileen!" "Eileen, would you stop by the store on the way home?" When she finally went to Mass at 5 P.M., Eileen was exhausted. Yet the whole day took on a new focus and meaning when she received communion. Hearing the words, "Eileen, the Body of Christ," she understood her whole day in a new light. The series of people calling her name had been Christ in a variety of disguises.

He blessed the bread . . . Blessings are unique to each person, and as numerous as the varieties of bread that feed the body: fragrance of French bread filling the house on a wintry day, sandwiches stuffed into lunch sacks, cinnamon rolls, pita, rye, blueberry muffins, Christmas breads braided and wreathed with raisins. Kneaded like yeast into life are the graces of family, education, faith, work, a web of sustaining relationships, the beauty of mornings that open like water lilies.

Each person should linger over a personal litany of blessings, both because it is individualized and because it is necessary to the next step. Before we are ever broken, we are blessed.

. . . **broke it** . . . Although Christ may not break us, he molds and shapes us, gives us grace to adapt. For proof we need only consider how our attitudes on controversial issues change over ten or twenty years. At another level, knowing that Jesus' body was initially broken into at least twelve pieces and now into countless more helps us see the holiness in our fragmented days and our divided hearts. Delving deeper, those who have entered their broken places and probed their wounds know them as sites of strength. In the spaces between the certainties, we find God.

When Miriam's son died, Jesus interrupted the funeral procession at Naim and rested his hand on the bier. The Jews considered it contaminated, but Jesus ignored the taboo to bring life. So he touches us in the places we rarely talk about, where we don't collect applause or awards, where we never brag. Even those things we are most ashamed of, he draws close and transforms into himself.

. . . **and gave it to them** . . . Women may shy away from the word "given" if we think of martyr types who have given themselves so utterly that they aren't even interesting, only bushed. We all know at least one: frazzled, fatigued, so busy meeting everyone else's needs that she neglects her own. We sound the alarm, "Codependent!" and run the other way.

Yet we are drawn to the vital, creative person who finds joy in the giving of herself. As a woman sits down to share a

meal into which she has poured time, she discovers the paradox. In nurturing others, she in turn is fed. The dancer and
the dance, the singer and the song become one. As Vince
Hovley, S.J., tells retreatants at Sacred Heart Jesuit Retreat
House: "Our Eucharist has the power to display our life's
inner meaning."

. . . saying "Take and eat, this is my body." It's an
indisputable fact of living enfleshed: where my body is, there
I am. In parenting, "This is my body" becomes a constant
refrain as time flows into launching healthy children: the but-
toning, unbuttoning, listening, combing, bathing, encouraging, chauffeuring, story-reading and tucking-in processes of
each day. Through the final, poignant letting go of grown
children, we say: "This is my body, my gift to the world. My
love, my energies, my failures and successes are poured into
this daughter or son who extends my life to others."

". . . This is my blood." Blood is both life-giving (the
blood donor) and life-draining (the battlefield wet with
blood). Such polarities can be embraced only by a symbol
moored in experience. When women gather to drink wine,
the occasion is often festive. As the chianti sparkles in the
glasses, the laughter bubbles. Sometimes, then, we segue into
the heartbreaks revealed only to the closest friends: the lost
loves, the tragic betrayals, the spouses and children who dis-
appoint, the talents wasted.

From the shared sorrow emerges a new strength. Because
we know the rocky twists of another's path, we can more
boldly walk our own. Our hearts ache for Julie, newly wid-
owed; Karen, undergoing a divorce; Linda, in chemothera-
phy; or Rosa, whose son is schizophrenic. Yet the mysterious
alchemy of friendship helps us bear our burdens, knowing
how bravely they carry theirs. In giving us the wine of his
blood, Jesus draws as close as companions splitting a bottle
of Chardonnay.

Because of their familiarity with blood, women have min-
imal squeamishness about it. Every month, menstruation has

a healthy, cleansing purpose. Blood gushes in childbirth, and in every subsequent scrape of childhood. We are used to wiping it off. We can even admire its red intensity: pulsing through artery and blushing in frail capillary. How could we circulate pale water? Without blood, we are lifeless. Separated from Christ, our lives turn vacuous. Cupped in his hands, we become chalices for others.

"Whenever you do this, remember me." Memory is crucial to the reflective life. Sometimes the only thing that keeps us going through silence is remembered song. While memory can be selective, it can also be insightful, revealing a meaning in retrospect that was missing from immediacy. When we seek concrete ways to remember Jesus, we grope for the look of his hands on bread and wine, the sound of his voice.

The two parts of his command, "When you do this, remember me," are like two hands clasping. The latter represents the kind of memory that triggered recognition of his presence at Emmaus. The former is our creation, the unique way we enact his words in our context. Thus, when we give ourselves as bread and wine to each other, we participate in an eternal process, old yet new.

Because of this eternal dimension, whatever we give is miraculously replenished. Perhaps we can best understand it by comparison to a creation in which the giver becomes the gift. Into the children we parent, the students we teach, the engines we tune, the patients we diagnose, the music we play, the gardens we tend—we pour ourselves. So Jesus' gift holds his heart; in offering ourselves, we remember him. We do even the most routine actions with the consecration of "a chosen race, a royal priesthood . . . a people claimed by God."

For Discussion or Reflection

1. Some women may not be accustomed to praying the Eucharistic prayer, but it is the unique birthright of a priestly people. What was your response to the meditation above? If you were able to enter into it, what helped

you do so?˙If you couldn't relate to it, what might have prevented you?

2. Quoting Robert Bellah, Nathan Mitchell points out in *Eucharist as Sacrament of Christian Initiation* that of the four verbs used in Mark's account of the Last Supper, two (taking and blessing) come from the world of masters; two (breaking and giving) belong to the world of scullery maids and servants. Washing feet and serving food were "women's work." Thus, "Jesus himself serves the meal, serves, like any housewife, the same meal to all including himself . . . . Long before Jesus was host, he was hostess."[2]

    Almost two thousand years after Jesus broke the traditional pattern of dominance/subordination, we still do not follow his example. (Indeed, we may flatten the effect by relegating the foot-washing to a ritual that clergy perform once a year, cozily removed from any bearing on real life. After the rite, the male clergy may smilingly process to a dinner prepared, served, and cleaned up by women!)

    Yet Jesus' actions liberate women who have been pressed into servile roles. As a wedge to understanding his service, imagine or name aloud a task someone could volunteer for you. (Whether or not someone has actually done it isn't the point. Dream.) Washing your hair? Scraping an icy car windshield? Ironing your blouse?

    Dream on. Imagine that the person who does this service stands a notch higher in the pecking order—perhaps the CEO making your morning coffee? Does the analogy to your own life help you appreciate what Jesus did?

    The Gospel hints at the security from which Jesus sailed past the social conventions: "Jesus, knowing that the Father had given all things into his hands, and that he had come from God and was going to God, got up from the table, took off his outer robe, and tied a towel around himself" (John 13:3–4). According to this passage, what motivates those who strive for mutuality in human relationships? How might the confidence of coming from God and going to God help teachers learn from their students, employers collaborate with employees, women and men recognize their interdependence, enjoy their partnerships, and refuse to exploit each other?

3. In *Meeting Jesus Again for the First Time*, Marcus Borg concurs that Jesus' treatment of women was striking for his era. Within his world, women were nobodies, disenfranchised, and radically separated from men in public life. Outside of the family setting, meals were men-only affairs; any women present there would have been perceived as courtesans.[3]

    The alternate vision Jesus proposed is seen in microcosm through the story of Deborah. He upsets her notions of how things "oughta be." The only precedent she knows is the role seized by the woman for whom she is named, the biblical giant Deborah. While gender divisions in contemporary U.S. society may not be as sharp, few would argue that women enjoy the freedom and opportunity accorded most men. Think of the obstacles women have encountered and overcome. Then reflect on what Jesus calls you to do. How does he invite you to enter a "discipleship of equals"? In the long haul to equality, where do you feel frustrated? Where affirmed?

4. In the Celtic tradition, no chore was performed without prayer. From the time a woman arose in the morning and kindled the fire to her last action of banking the peat at night, each action was done with a blessing. Milking the cow, churning the butter, making the cloth were rituals

performed with full attention and prayerfulness. Esther
de Waal records in *Every Earthly Blessing* the blessing as
cloth was made for the family:

> This is not cloth for priest or cleric
> But it is cloth for my own little Donald of love,
> For my companion beloved, for John of joy,
> And for Muriel of loveliest hue.[4]

Making beer, the women would ask that Jesus join their
cheerful drinking: "I would like a great lake of beer/ For
the King of Kings."[5]

Perhaps such single-minded attention is impossible
in an age of fragmentation. Knowing how easily he can
become distracted, John Kavanaugh compares his work
to that of Martha: at times resentful and egotistical; at
other times, joyful and relaxed. On better days, he
writes in "Working and Wanting," (*America,* July 15,
1995): "I can go about my tasks knowing that they, too,
are the presence of God. My work is no longer something exacted of me, toil grudgingly given. Rather, it
flows freely, a display of how good it is to be alive, to be
here, to be now."

How do you see your own work? Does blessing
enter into it, or does it seem like unrelieved drudgery, a
planet away from your spiritual life? In what ways might
it be possible to draw the two together? According to
the Rule of St. Benedict, garden tools, pots, or pans
should be treated with as much care as sacred altar vessels. Perhaps we need blessings for computers, micro-
waves, phones, and fax machines, just as for beer vats or
weaving looms. Write or pray aloud a blessing for the
tools you use most often:

5. Anthropologist Mary Catherine Bateson chooses the concept of sacrament to show how it is possible to "create a context of sharing with very simple material cues." Jesus didn't prepare an elaborate, four-course meal, but chose relatively simple bread and wine for Communion. In so doing, he gives women a direction. As Bateson writes in *Composing a Life*: "We might be better off if we could separate food as nourishment and pleasure from food as the currency of care that leaves so many women laboring long hours to prove affection in that semantic muddle called nurturance."[6]

    She goes on to draw a lesson from the elaborate ritual of infant feeding during the 1940s and 1950s—washing, sterilizing, rigidly scheduling bottles—before the rediscovery of breast-feeding's simplicity. The material signs of affection still carry an important message, but how might you simplify or delegate the tasks that have become onerous? How might you use your time and talent more creatively?

15

Esther

Accosts Peter

(MATT. 26:69–75; MARK 14:66–72;
LUKE 22:54–62; JOHN 18:15–18)

She knows the burly silhouette
against the bonfire. Blared on
his face the unmistakable identity,
echoed in the bramble of his words.

She finds voice, hangs a banner to
welcome him home: You were with him.
Expecting he'll shout "Yes!", find
himself, abandon the fire's warm curve.

His words burn worse than thorns.
His hulking shadow blots her light
as he spits venom, cursing the friend
tortured while they toast their hands.

The firelight a flush on her cheekbones,
she persists. If he abandons one, can he
desert the fine companions who ate and fished
and puzzled and roared their jokes together?

Surely you were one of them! Another bitter oath,
rapier of the unarmed man. Recognition flares in
her eyes; she is not so easily fooled. Still she
challenges Peter; even now the cock crows betrayal.

It had to be him. The first time I identified Peter, I
thought I might be mistaken because it was so dark in the
courtyard, and my vision isn't the sharpest. But then I heard
him talk. Living in Jerusalem, a cosmopolitan city, I've devel-
oped a good ear for accents. His speech pegged him a
Galilean, as surely as the smell of fish in his clothes or the
rope burns on his hands marked him a fisherman.

For a few deluded moments, I thought I'd offer him an
opportunity. I didn't know why he'd denied his friend, but
I'd give him a second chance to reclaim the tie, shift into himself again. It would be simple as opening a door—and that's
my job. "Come home, Peter!" I'd say, with the ease of calling
my children home at dusk. "Your show is preposterous; no
one believes you anyway, so drop your disguise!" Then we'd
all have a good laugh at his lousy acting ability.

But he only got nastier. Maybe it was the tension of wondering what was going on in Caiphas's palace. Behind those
smooth marble walls lurked dank cells, thugs with meaty
fists, and tortures no one talked about. Did Peter bluster
loudly to cover the moaning of victims? Did we huddle close
to the fire's crackling because we feared the silence?

The conviction was growing in me that if I did not speak
up, I was an unwitting participant in the ordeal of an innocent person. I'd seen Jesus when they dragged him in; one
exhausted man with all the authorities massed against him. I
stood alone too, knowing it was impossible to tackle the
whole court, the bloodthirsty assembly of priests and elders.
But at least I could confront the fisherman before me. My

piece was a tiny chip in a vast mosaic, but I could do my part. My name, after all, is Esther.

Just the mention of the brave queen kindles my courage. On every feast of Purim, I had heard her story; by now it had sunk bone-deep. I remembered the message Mordecai sent her, as she stood on the threshold, poised to preserve the Hebrew people from slaughter: "Who knows? Perhaps you have come to the throne for just such a time as this" (Esther 4:14).

That chilly courtyard was no throne room, but the summons was the same. The whole Jewish people had been jeopardized then; one man was in danger now. Esther had had time for careful planning. I had a few minutes for a quick challenge. But I called upon her spirit and dived in as if her motto waved above me: "And if I perish, I perish" (Esther 4:16).

The third time, I spoke in a tone that surprised me with its surety. "You are one of them." My words shimmered in the smoky air. If he would turn from one friend, surely he could not forget the whole company! From what I'd heard, anyone would be honored to be part of that crowd. People who had felt the healing touch or heard the welcoming word flocked from all over the countryside to be near them. Surely a man who had been so close to that life for so long would admit it! What was he afraid of?

Me, I guess. His venom poured on me as though I'd caused his dilemma. I have heard plenty of curses, but he vomited these with a filthy, destructive force. Stunned, I fled from the courtyard into the night air. Even the cool dampness was preferable to sharing the firelight with such poison. Breathing heavily, I looked up at the sky and remembered that Esther means "star." Her light made my failure seem more miserable. On the horizon, a pale dawn was glowing. The day's bustle would soon begin; in a nearby yard, a cock's crow broke the last few moments of quiet night. I gritted my teeth and muttered, "So I'm not a queen like you. I didn't save anyone. But I tried."

ESTHER TODAY

Just as in a poem, a dream or a parable, our understanding of this story may be enhanced by taking the roles of all the characters, regardless of their gender. Much as we may want to identify with Esther, we also suspect that the worm which coiled in Peter also squirms deep in ourselves. First, let's reflect on Esther's challenge to Peter. Today we might call this process of summoning courage to articulate a deeply held belief "finding voice."

Women's Ways of Knowing by Mary Belenky and others traces this process, which begins in passive silence and ends in autonomous speech. In the early phases, women accept the stereotype: "Conventional feminine goodness means being voiceless as well as selfless."[1] They submit unquestioningly to authority, and in the worst cases, prefer even abuse to independence. Gradually, some come to perceive the reliability of their own inner voices. The movement from external to internal authority is pivotal: "The interior voice has become . . . the hallmark of women's emergent sense of self and sense of agency and control."[2]

Esther trusts the authority of the inner voice. We can tell from her boldness as she insists, "You were with him," and ignores Peter's rebuffs. While she wants to speak truth, Peter walls off dialogue with repeated denial and cursing.

Today, women still challenge Peter, if we see him as a symbol for the institutional church. Women initiate a movement beyond old agendas, exhausted paradigms, unsuccessful policies. Because women have so little power, they have the freedom to protest forthrightly when images and language become too narrow. They invite males to explore their feminine sides, enjoy their emotions, and exercise their compassion. A flowering in feminist theology, ritual, and art has attested to the Spirit's presence in the movement and underscored the fact that any community which excludes women impoverishes itself. St. Teresa of Avila once said, "Let's not imagine that we are hollow inside,"[3] and women are just starting to tap the power of that vast inner treasure.

With sexual discrimination still rampant, many churches that could help liberate only continue to enslave. A religious framework that once satisfied has become a cage because it is imposed from without, univocally. Miriam Therese Winter and co-authors record in *Defecting in Place* the distress of women in all religious traditions:

- "My child is harassed by children from other traditions because his mother 'thinks she is a minister.'"[4]

- "It just seemed screamingly unjust to tell [my daughter] that her brother could become a priest but she couldn't."[5]

- "Participating in my church worship made me feel dead, sad . . . I go to church on Sunday and it takes me all week to recover."[6]

Because of the failure of the Catholic Church to fully include women in ordained ministry, it has become a locus for challenges to Peter. While many Catholic women are finding voice, Joan Chittister, O.S.B., serves as one outstanding spokeswoman. She says loudly and clearly that two thousand years after Jesus, his intention of welcoming women has not been satisfied. He missioned the Samaritan women, Mary, and the women at the tomb to preach the good news; in many dioceses today, women are forbidden to preach the gospel. Chittister underscores the irony of people hungry for the sacraments, while women are denied ordination. Women like Chittister may be hounded by pickets, but they stand in a long tradition of speaking the truth to power, even to a formidable hierarchy. They have scriptural precedents. They draw their strength from women like Esther.

The Episcopal Church was ambivalent about the role of women even after the General Convention approved the

"Philadelphia 11," women ordained in 1974. The official recognition came after two grueling years of "controversy and rejection approaching psychological excommunication."[7] Carter Heyward, one of the group, explained why she was ordained: a belief that the power of Christ came not from his masculinity, but from his humanness, in which women share. She concludes, "The power of the Risen Christ in history cannot be confined to fathers and sons."[8]

The question of equality is larger than ordination: ordained women of many traditions are still marginalized; underpaid; assigned small, rural parishes; dismissed or devalued in decision-making processes. Female members of the Church of the Brethren, while able to be ordained, have struggled for over a hundred years to change the name of their congregation. Authoritarian leadership, obsession with control, male-dominated rites, and exclusive language persist in the "patriarchal stew." Mary Daly's 1973 dictum continues to ring true: "If God is male, then the male is God."[9]

Yet, women's efforts to achieve mutuality and equality, foster justice, explore women's spirituality and find alternate forms of worship have risen like leaven in individual denominations, while at the same time blurring rigid denominational identities. As women create a new order, they celebrate the gift of being female and act out their belief that the Spirit sings within them.

One woman interviewed by Winter and her co-authors of *Defecting in Place* expressed the paradox of their position: "Am I angry? You bet! Am I conflicted? You bet! Am I committed to *living* Eucharist, sharing what we're given, in gratitude? You bet!"[10] Exploring new territory, they are pioneers making it up as they go along. At the same time they remain, like biblical women, the keepers of the memories, the guardians of the heart's traditions.

ℒ♥

PETER TODAY

However, if we identify too smugly and self-righteously with the voices of oppressed women, we can fail to learn from Peter's mistake. Esther may have left the courtyard feeling like a failure, but he plodded away as a betrayer. His identity is written on his face, engraved in his speech patterns, marked so indelibly that even the casual observer knows he is a friend of Jesus. The only problem is his failure to recognize himself. Human beings are the only species that can either affirm or deny their own nature. No cheetah clocks its speed; no lion regrets its voracious appetite; no frog commits suicide. The consciousness unique to humans can be a blessing or a curse. When Peter deserts Jesus, the vehemence of his betrayal is a clue that their friendship is crucial to his identity. According to Mark, "He started calling down curses on himself" (14:71).

Women today often fail to recognize what is most true for their deepest selves. Within us throbs a strong desire for identity, which if frustrated, leads to agony. Yet we act from vanity ("Of course I can be Supermom—work two jobs, keep the house immaculate, run the hospital volunteer program, *and* bake cookies for the potluck!"), and wonder why we're too tired to savor our achievements. On a continuous quest for "more," we race through the only life we have.

As Clarissa Pinkola Estes points out repeatedly in *Women Who Run with the Wolves*, we neglect our creative life, our instinctual self, or our true love only at our peril. Schooled to politeness, we say yes too quickly to the noble cause, and bypass the key question: Is this project right for me at this time? Sometimes our refusal to act stems from fear of failure, the paralysis that insists on perfection in every detail. Unconsciously, we may allow the people closest to us too much influence over decisions that are rightly ours. (Was Peter, for instance, swayed by peer pressure, the grating awareness that his other friends had fled? Was he afraid to lose status with Esther?)

Yet an inner authority over who I am and where I am going is essential to the faithful life. At a time when all other religious writers warned that the self should be repressed, disciplined, and "tamed," St. Ignatius Loyola described God's will not as an external norm to which people must conform, but an internal voice. The Spirit within leads to our good; when I am in tune with that Spirit, I am in God. Continuing that tradition, the Ignatian exercises still begin with the question, "What is your deepest desire?" When we have identified that longing, we can act in accord with the Creator's design for our nature, moving toward good and truth.[11]

Furthermore, when we act from that deep center, we discover the freedom of God's children. We end the exhausting search for the one right choice among thousands, knowing that God provides a multiplicity of fine opportunities. We no longer grovel to placate a tyrannous master; we respect our own instincts. As William Lynch asks in *Images of Hope*: "Why not wish greatly and go forward boldly, if God wills it so?"[12]

While Peter's choice of respectable anonymity over his deepest desire is cowardly and contradictory, his mistake still provides a "teaching moment." We learn from him that even a bald betrayal does not mean the end. While he weeps bitterly over his denial, it does not sever his relationship with Christ. In fact, some people speculate that Jesus deliberately chose a man with a huge propensity for error as the founder of his church! No matter how miserable our failure, it gives us a new angle on the next decision. Peter does not beat himself up; if anything, he develops a deeper friendship with Jesus whom he betrayed.

This "healing of memories" is clear in the post-Resurrection account of Peter diving into the sea, naked, after

John identifies a stranger on the shore, preparing breakfast and telling them where to cast their fishing nets (John 21:1–19). Similarities in the story show how "a broken past can resurface and be redeemed."[13] Once again the air filled with the aroma of the charcoal fire. Peter's threefold denial parallels his profession of love, also repeated three times.

For Peter as for women like Susanna and Magda, things can come miraculously full circle.

FOR DISCUSSION AND REFLECTION

1. Many women plant themselves squarely in the face of authority and declare, "You're wrong."

    *   What do you admire in these women?

    *   What about them makes you uncomfortable?

    *   Do you ever challenge authority, perhaps in more subtle ways? How?

2. Reenact the confrontation between Esther and Peter (Matt. 26:69–75; Mark 14:66–72; Luke 22:54–62; John 18:15–18) in whatever form appeals to you: Dance, drawing, mime, sculpture, role-playing or expanding their dialogue in writing. In the version above, she feels she has failed. Would you agree or disagree? Why was her challenge to Peter so important that all four Gospels record it?

    Then imagine Esther meeting Peter a year later, as he preaches boldly in the porticos of the temple. Using the same form, or choosing a different one of your own, create their conversation.

    Despite the poison of their initial meeting, it is important that Esther and Peter stay in dialogue. Richard Rohr points out that when two sides justify their own excesses because they are required by the excesses of the other side, then the *via media,* or golden mean, is lost.[14]

For balanced conversation, people need common ground where they can meet as human beings seeking truth together—not as entrenched armies.

Do you think that some women and some church leaders have become so distanced, so polarized that dialogue between them has become impossible? If so, why has this occured, and how could the situation be changed? If not, what signs of hope do you see? On what common ground does dialogue still flourish? What women and men within your denomination do you look to for leadership? How do they keep the channels of communication open?

3. Allow the Ignatian question to resonate through the week ahead: "What is your deepest desire?" How does keeping that question in the forefront of your mind shape your days or affect your attitudes and behaviors?

4. Address a prayer or a letter to Esther and/or Peter. Do you find some of them both in yourself? Why was their meeting probably not an accident, but part of the divine design? In your prayer or letter, describe a situation when you felt called to speak out on an issue.

5. Each version of this incident has details none of the others have. If it suits your style, choose one or more of these to reflect on or discuss:

   • Mark has Peter "burst into tears" when he recalls Jesus' prediction of his betrayal—the phrase we might use for a child.

   • Luke records that after his third denial, "the Lord turned and looked straight at Peter." Jesus also looked directly at the people he called to follow him. What is in that look?

   •. Matthew says Peter "went outside and wept bitterly,"

a subtle comment on his separation from the warmth
of human community.

- John calls the maid servant (Esther) the keeper of
  the door. Beyond the literal meaning, what else
  could this symbolize?

16

Claudia,
Wife of Pontius Pilate

(MATTHEW 27:19)

The tension between them
old as Eden. He knew her
history: her intuition
hit target, snapping like
iron trap on truth when
his logic failed.

He usually ignored her, but
she'd sounded his own doubt.
Known for quick, decisive
sentences, he'd engaged this
criminal in conversation.
Purple oddly fit the man.

He rehearsed excuses: he had tried,
words flimsy dikes against the tidal
jeering: reason held hostage by mob.
Her dream could not have stayed them,
slight paper in a torrential sea.
He washed his hands in a tepid bowl.

She loved their villa, a secure post.
So he acted to protect her! Even as he
fantasized, her patrician back turned.
His ideals slid into unmarked graves.
Nagging itch, a voice he could not
drown whispered she was right.

In the billowy cloud of dream, one thing was constant: that face. I kept trying to get closer, but in a dreamy way, I slogged through quicksand. I had seen him somewhere before, perhaps on the streets of Jerusalem, but had not attached much importance to yet another itinerant preacher. The locals crowded around him, hoping to relieve the dreariness of their days. I assumed he was simply the diversion of the moment. It's funny about dreams: details we dismiss casually during waking hours assume an enormous importance in the shadowy world.

On awakening, I tried to shake it off, but the face haunted my day. I turned to other affairs, concentrated on more pressing things, and became annoyed that this dream assumed so much weight. We had an empire to run: how could that colossal mechanism be brought to its knees by a tiny grain of sand?

What troubled me most was how the pressing particularity of that face eroded my comfortable assumptions. "The Jews," "the rebels," "the native peoples"—those were the politer terms employed in the palace, but probably not used in the barracks. We referred to them scornfully as a collective to be tamed, an annoying problem to be solved. Now "they" had taken on a face filled with sadness.

I was shocked that the face was not leering like a demon, nor sneering with hatred at the occupying power. That face was lovable, as noble as my father's, as sensitive as my brother's.

It was irritating to feel the floor shifting beneath my feet. But the dream's tone of fear was worse: blood had permeated my dream, the blood of the innocent splashing on Pilate and staining his hands. Nothing I could do would wash it off, though I floated across mosaic floors, bringing cool pitchers of water scented with rose. Some mysterious danger lurked here, threatening all we held most dear.

I had no alternative but to send Pilate a warning. My husband was powerful; he commanded a legion; surely he could resist some rabid religious leaders, some petty local bureaucrats! But to be absolutely certain, I cut my words clearly—no ambiguity, no qualifications, clean as the straight line chiseled down a marble column: "Have nothing to do with that man." Pilate wasn't the only one who could issue an imperial order!

When he returned from the trial, I expected everything to be settled. Surely he would enact such a lucid message!

"It's not so simple, Claudia," Pilate muttered, and I knew he didn't want to discuss it. "I am innocent of that man's blood." He attempted his usual authority, but the words rang hollow. The tragic delusion of the powerful—they think that by saying something, they can make it so! Even the gesture he described, the pathetic attempt to wash his hands in front of the bloodthirsty mob, was unconvincing. "Oh Pilate," I winced, remembering my dream of blood that the Mediterranean itself could not have cleansed. I have never been so disappointed in his cowardice. By contrast, the face of my dream seemed to contain all the courage in the world.

CLAUDIA TODAY

Only Matthew records, in thirty-eight words, the dream of Pilate's wife. Perhaps because it is so brief, the story appeals to the imagination to fill it out.

The first intriguing note is its echo of the biblical and Roman tradition of the dream. Abraham, Joseph, and the

Magi all had dreams (today we might call them insights) that brought them truth. Yet the men were able to act on their intuitions, and have been honored ever since for their trust. The frustration for Claudia must have been that she could act only through an intermediary, Pilate, who ultimately fails to put her vision into practice. In this sense, she is more like Julius Caesar's wife, Calpurnia, who warned her husband not to go to the Forum on the Ides of March because she had dreamed about his wounded and bloody corpse. He ignored her warning, and was subsequently betrayed and murdered.

We know that few Roman women of Claudia's time enjoyed autonomy. In the classical period, they had no decision-making authority or leadership. The authors of the *Women's Bible Commentary* believe that Luke, trying to make Christianity acceptable to the "public forum of the empire, the world of men," blurs "traditional and historical traces of women's leadership and exaggerates the leadership by men."[1] The expanded role Jesus had given women in his community would be suspect in the Roman world, hence Jesus' innovation was de-emphasized.

Another intriguing thing about the story is that sharp divisions aren't drawn along gender lines. Some of Claudia spills into Pilate; and vice-versa. He must follow protocol, but so must she. She cannot approach him directly, but must send a messenger. That intermediary step must have grated, but she knew the system and worked within it. We bemoan the hierarchies we must face—until we compare them to the structure of the Roman empire, a precise organization that had subdued most of the known world! Into that complex, ordered system, Claudia introduces a glitch, like the bug that devastates advanced technology. Such a human thing, shadowy and insubstantial as a dream is flimsy evidence, hardly admissable in court proceedings, easily mocked in a trial.

The amazing thing is the credence Pilate gives it. Perhaps his wife confirmed his own suspicion. In several maneuvers, he distances himself from the shabby proceedings. Or perhaps he tries to follow her advice, "Have nothing to do with this man." Pilate recognizes the jealous motivation driving the priests and elders who had handed Jesus over. He gives the crowd the choice of which prisoner to release: Jesus or Barabbas? In the governor's words, "What harm has he done?" may be an effort to heed Claudia's warning. Pilate's final attempt to evade responsibility comes in the denial: "I am innocent of this man's blood. It is your concern." Washing his hands symbolizes his attitude of "It's not my problem." The gesture echoes Claudia, who also proposes a "hands off" policy.

While she certainly does not win a victory, Claudia represents loyalty in the face of betrayal. Although Pilate capitulated from fear of the mob, she spoke loud and clear. Later Christian tradition has named her "Claudia Procula," or follower at the gate; the Greek Orthodox Church canonized her, and celebrates her feast October 27.

FOR REFLECTION OR DISCUSSION

1. While the poem represents one scenario that may have happened when Pilate came home, what actually happened is certainly open to individual interpretation. Picture the scene in your own mind: the queenly woman in the palatial setting, the powerful man, the dangerous issue hanging in the air between them. The fate of Jesus was a complex question, with political overtones and moral ambiguities that surface throughout Pilate's conversations with him. Recreate the dialogue between Claudia and Pilate.

2. "You've got to be carefully taught," goes the song from *South Pacific*, "to hate all the people your relatives hate." Have you ever experienced the coming to insight expressed here by Claudia, when a collective we once

dismissed as "the other" suddenly takes on the particularity of a single human face? Did it happen in terms of a different ethnic group, socioeconomic class, religious tradition, political party, school of thought? What difference does this insight make in your life now?

3. Like many of the hidden women described in this book, Claudia may never have received any assurance that what she was doing was right. Her voice, like Esther's confronting Peter, may have seemed weak as a whisper in the passion narratives which grind inexorably to their savage conclusion. Yet those voices which seemed to fail speak loudly to us. What do they say about ambiguity? About the transformations wrought by time? About the unreliability of appearances?

4. Jung believed that dreams carried important messages from the unconscious. Some people think dreams are messengers of God. How much importance do you give your own dreams? Are they an untapped resource for understanding your psyche, or do you think they are overrated?

17

Hannah

at the Foot of the Cross

(MARK 15:40–41)

The baby's weight inside me was as heavy as the atmosphere around me. The other women had scoffed at my coming: someone seven months pregnant didn't belong at an execution! But Mary Magdalene understood why I needed to be there; I could look to her support as I had before.

I remember telling Mary I was pregnant. Not a word of condemnation came from her, not a single hint of disappointment or disapproval. I didn't want to remember how it happened, how quickly the father disappeared, or how I had betrayed my parents' trust. I will always be thankful that Mary didn't ask for any details, didn't waste a minute on the past. She just looked ahead, bubbly and excited, planning for the future as though this were her grandchild. Her enthusiasm spilled over, rousing me from dullness. We started choosing names, making blankets and clothing. Every tiny stitch I took brought a kind of balm, healing the rejection that throbbed inside, eroding the terrible aloneness.

While we planned and sewed, she told stories. "Something marvelous is afoot, my dear," she used to whisper as though we were conspirators. "Aren't we the lucky ones to be living now? And what a treasure for your baby! To be born into this little circle of support, to know Jesus and his friends: a fine inheritance for a wee one!" I began to believe her: if they welcomed my child as warmly as they had me—without a trace of judgment—then my baby would have a family. I felt secure that they would never call the little one a bastard.

Then it was all ruined. Our high hopes dashed, our buoyant optimism smothered, that marvelous potential spoiled. It was as if someone had wiped the stars from the sky, or smashed the mountains into a flat streak against the horizon.

When they dragged Jesus onto the hill, I thought I would vomit. Welts swelled on his back, blood matted his hair, spittle trailed through the filth on his cheeks. Worse than the hatred that seethed around him was the sadness enveloping him. I couldn't watch, but I heard the hammer blows, the splintering noise as they hoisted the cross aloft, the curses of the soldiers, his moaning.

All we could do through this brutal business engineered by politicians and rabbis was look on passively. In my rage, wanting to lash out, I forgot I was pregnant and pleaded hysterically with Mary, "Can't we do something? Tell them to stop!" But it just dragged on, as though they had a job to do and would finish it, no matter how horrible the task. If they overlook the nasty fact that this is a human being, people can do anything, I guess.

Then Mary reminded me that Jesus had something to accomplish too. She murmured low, in a desperate effort to comfort me or reassure herself, what he'd said the night before. There in the draining heat, with dust clogging our nostrils, our emotions spent and the awful shadow looming above us, she retrieved the memory. "So this is what he meant!" she breathed. "A woman in childbirth suffers because her time has come."

Immediately she had my attention. Had Jesus thought of me? Somehow he knew that terrible mixture of emotions warring inside: dread and hope, fear and anticipation, bravery and embarrassment, outrage and blessing.

Whenever I think of the Hannah for whom I am named, I am so ashamed. Almost her whole married life waiting for a child, all her attention bent on that potential, her prayer straining with hope, her ardent pleading unrewarded, the grieving at the sight of other children, the insults she endured, then her life wrapped around the son, her sacrifice of Samuel as a gift to our whole people . . .

I didn't deserve to bear her name. In painful contrast, I resented the baby; I fought the idea of motherhood; I resisted the motion within; I wished with all my heart that the pregnancy had never happened. Only with Mary Magdalene, who seemed to know about inner torment, could I reach any peace.

Mary was still talking. "Don't you see, Hannah? He dreaded this day. But at the same time, it's his whole reason for being. He must see beyond Calvary. So you will look past the labor to the baby's safe deliverance."

She had more faith in me than I did. I was likely to sink into the pain and never get beyond the bloody ordeal. But her confidence inspired me to look at the scene I'd avoided, even see its connection to me. The baby, round and innocent within; the man stretched taut, and just as innocent, above. Any normal person would shield the eyes, draw a cloak close in self-protection, retreat to a distance in self-defense.

But Mary, as usual, insisted we stand fast. She started me thinking: could this death scene conceal mysterious birth pains? Did my condition, such an enormous liability, sensitize me to the link between a torture victim and a birthing mother? Were his convulsions as life-giving as my contractions would be?

I'd been tired and crabby for seven months. Throughout that stretch of time, I'd done almost nothing. Without Mary's encouragement, I wouldn't have had the energy to make a few shirts and diapers. But maybe my life force was pouring in a different direction. I didn't seem to be doing much; but I was creating ears, eyes, fingers, a heart, chin, and mouth. My flesh given to nurture another's, my blood circulating into the child's system: hadn't Jesus said something about "my body and blood, given for you"?

The risk that lies ahead, the pain I will endure seem cast in a different light now. From the ashes of disaster, new seeds can sprout. Jesus gave me the right to be afraid, and the hope to get me through. I know that I can be sad, but also steady. If I can let go of anger and forgive as he did, I will clear the proper space for a baby to be born. How strange that I should learn from a dying man how to give birth.

Hannah Today

The sentimentality surrounding pregnancy and childbirth can conceal less pleasant realities. Every child won't be a cherub; every mother doesn't glow with rosy health; and contrary to the greeting cards, every family isn't convinced that the little darling is a blessing. Even the most welcome, planned pregnancy and long-awaited birth is shrouded with ambivalence.

Yes, a mother may think, I want this baby, but will I survive labor and delivery? Will the child be healthy? How will my life change? How much of myself must I surrender to nurture this new life? How will the infant's demands affect my other relationships? If middle-class North American women, who often have competent medical care and high tech hospital facilities, worry about childbirth, what of the countless women who give birth in squalor, without medical aid, to undernourished babies that are the result of rape or incest, and place another unwanted burden on a family that is already strapped?

And yet, women continue to give birth. Mothers have always loved the potential of their children's lives enough to risk their own. Perhaps they are captivated by the promise, the radiant possibility.

To the difficult births in less than ideal conditions, Jesus' pain brings a new dimension. Marie-Eloise Rosenblatt writes, "In the passion, Jesus shares the vulnerability women feel in society."[1] He is voiceless in judicial proceedings, as women often are, and powerless to prevent violence, as women often are. Much as women hate to feel like passive victims, we often are. Blind to accomplishments that are remarkable, women often believe they have done little, because the standards of achievement are male-defined. Where in the Gross National Product do we ever calculate the birth of a healthy human being? How in a resume do we include the launching of a secure child?

For those who are not biological mothers, or who have passed that stage, pregnancy takes on different connotations. That mysterious process of giving life may become the nurture of other relationships, a creative work, or the birthing of a new self. As with the physical condition, this state may be exhausting and debilitating, the results impossible to predict.

Yet, women's waiting participates in God's gestation; our creative processes enflesh the divine. Through pregnancy in its myriad forms, we learn first-hand about the interconnectedness of all life. Furthermore, experiences of birthing give women a unique perspective on the cross. Like Hannah and Mary Magdalene, we have an intimate understanding of what transpired on Calvary. In the words of poet Jessica Powers, "Nothing but pain could go to meet this love."[2]

FOR DISCUSSION OR REFLECTION

1. "And there were many other women there who had come up to Jerusalem with him." (Mark 15:41)

    •   How do you feel about the fact that the women stayed faithful to Jesus, even to the bitter end, while all the men except John fled?

- What does it mean to you that Jesus chose a feminine metaphor of giving birth to describe our salvation, our arduous birth into eternal life?

2. Christ's message came to Hannah through Mary Magdalene. Who has served as such a channel for you? What experiences has your mentor had that have enabled him or her to convey Jesus' word with understanding and clarity? What have you learned from this model about being Christ-like without being preachy, phony, or pious?

3. Mark's community saw the cross as an instrument of political terrorism inflicted by the ruling Roman power on violent criminals, slaves, and people without rights. Only in more recent eras has the cross been embellished with jewels, cast in silver and gold, and worn as jewelry. As Jim Dunning points out in Echoing God's Word, that trivialization would seem to the first Christians like hanging a tiny electric chair on a gold chain around the neck.[3]

   Does knowing the evolution of a primary Christian symbol affect your attitude toward it? A Venezuelan artist has sculpted a crucifix with a pregnant woman hanging from it. What do you think of this adaptation? If the crucifix has lost some of its significance for you, what image might work better? Create your own symbol of death/new life.

4. The fourteenth-century mystic Julian of Norwich knew that contemplating suffering could be burdensome. She proposed instead that Jesus' passion was his work; he would work even harder if necessary, to accomplish his task. Perhaps a contemporary metaphor might be a woman who brings home her pay check to meet her family's needs. Knowing that her work has provided their education, medical care, piano lessons or clothing, she is

well compensated. If she had to work harder to finance a special need, she would probably do it.

Julian imagined Jesus saying, "Art thou well paid that I suffered for thee? . . . If thou art paid, I am paid. It is a joy, a bliss and an endless liking to me that ever I suffered passion for thee. And if I could suffer more, I would suffer more."[4]

Jesus looks from the cross at you. He is pleased with what you have done to continue his work and express his love, especially with:

John Kavanaugh writes in *America* (April 1, 1995) that Jesus, looking on you with love from the cross, says now and eternally: "Yes, you needed this. And yes, you were worth it." How do both thoughts apply to yourself?

5. Mothers are at their best when they are in touch with the source of all maternal love, God. When we are tempted to self-sufficiency, arrogance or despair, it may help to remember that God is continually giving birth to us, that in God's arms we are vulnerable children. Read Psalm 131 prayerfully.

The First Resurrection Appearance

Defiant as child who refuses
to let the story close sadly,
she mined it again, hunting
the first page for a clue
that would foretell calamity.

Did this abrupt and brutal end
lurk in the promise of endless reign?
Her welcome had brought the baby and
all blessing. Limp as long
grasses, he lay in her arms.

If she squinted, the welts
and nail marks diappeared.
She could cradle the infant, soothe,
pretend the quilt was never rent
nor song stifled, nor son crucified.

Her dream was Easter-interrupted.
Again, that presence stirred,
familiar as cloak on peg,
scent of cedar or door ajar,
the signs of son come home.

She laughed at tragedy ending well,
loved him fiercely for trouncing death,
twisting the plot, flooding a cavernous
tomb with light, dancing age into youth,
frost into blossom, end into beginning.

18

Joanna's
"Idle Tale"

(LUKE 24:1–13)

I could barely sleep, the morning's errand looming over the night. A monstrous boulder dominated my dreams, and I felt crushed beneath its weight, grazing my knuckles against its flinty surface. That night followed the least restful, most nerve-wracking Sabbath I'd ever spent. Any "holy" thoughts were lost in wondering about the dank tomb, the stench, the violence we might face the next morning.

For the tenth time, I checked the supplies: Cloths and spices, balm for that broken body. Would we have enough? Would the guards stop us? Would everyone who'd agreed to come show up? Could we budge the stone? Maybe I stewed over the little questions so I could suppress the larger one: how could a tomb contain *him*, his vibrant, pulsing life?

My friends looked exhausted too when we gathered in the greyness before dawn. We'd all had a sleepless night and longed to begin the day, no matter how terrible it might be. Something stronger than our questions drove us to the sad task ahead. Maybe it was the memory of his arm hanging limply from the rock-hewn shelf, the bruises in his hand turning violet. Maybe it was his insistence at our last meal together: remember me. Maybe it was the look on his mother's face when we wrapped the torn limbs in linen. Each of us bore different memories, like shadowy companions along the road.

From a distance, I thought the stone loomed larger and darker than I'd remembered. But as I got closer, I realized it wasn't a boulder but a dark opening, a glaring hole. Our pace quickened. Was I hallucinating, or did glimmers of white flash inside? I grasped Mary Magdalene's hand for courage as we stepped into the cool tomb. We barely had time to blink our eyes and adjust to the darkness before we heard a voice buoyant with song.

For the rest of my life I will carry those words, "Why do you look for the living among the dead? He is not here, but has risen." Would every sadness unravel so swiftly? Would our sharpest tragedies be robbed of their sting? If someone told me then that paralytics could dance, trees could hoist themselves into the sea, and the dead could sing, I'd believe it. My inner terrain has shifted somehow.

And the men who scoff at us? They've just missed the best news they could ever hear, poor fools.

JOANNA TODAY

Joanna's experience rings true to the words of Psalm 30:

> Weeping may linger for the night
> but joy comes with the morning.

Since Jesus rose from the dead, all the "little r" resurrections of our lives share in his Resurrection. While we can be sad, we cannot be hopeless. Because the tomb was empty, we are called to trust beyond dead-ended appearances. Gazing grimly into any black hole, faith remembers that the stone has forever been rolled away. Surprising reversals can spring from that which appeared to be lost.

Paradoxically, whispers of resurrection swell most persistently in the places we least expect to hear them. For instance, El Salvador, notorious scene of brutal death squad activity is also fertile ground for new life. In *Companions of Jesus*, Jon Sobrino, S.J., writes of four North American women murdered there:

> I have stood by the bodies of Maura Clarke, Ita Ford, Dorothy Kazel, and Jean Donovan. . . . The murdered Christ is here in the person of four women. . . . Christ lies dead here among us. He is Maura, Ita, Dorothy, and Jean. But he is risen too in these same four women, and he keeps the hope of liberation alive.

> Salvation comes to us through all women and men who love truth more than lies, who are more eager to give than to receive, and whose love is that supreme love that gives life rather than keeping it for oneself. Yes, their dead bodies fill us with sorrow and indignation. And yet our last word must be: Thank you.[1]

Sobrino's words would prove prophetic. On November 15, 1989, Elba Ramos, who was the cook for Sobrino and his Jesuit community at the University of Central America, washed her best dress and gave it to a woman displaced by the bombing. Such lavish generosity was typical of Elba, whose poverty could not dim her buoyant good humor, nor quiet her laughter.

The next day, she was martyred. Her last gesture was flinging her leg across her daughter Celina, shot at her side. Elba's husband subsequently planted six red roses for the Jesuits, two yellow ones for his wife and daughter. Now as they bloom on ground once wet with blood, they echo that Resurrection scene of Mary meeting Christ in a garden.

Rumors of resurrection abound in our time and country as well. One September, a class of first grade children planted a "time capsule." Each parent wrote a letter to each child, expressing their hopes for the new year. The teacher planned to dig up the capsule in the spring, as a catalyst for review of the year.

During a January blizzard, the father of a girl named Pilar was killed in an auto accident. With the grieving that ensued, the teacher forgot about the time capsule. But when she unearthed it in May, she found the long and beautiful letter Pilar's daddy had written her in the fall. She phoned the mother; all three read the letter with a mixture of tears and joy. On two lined sheets of loose-leaf, he had come alive again.

Almost as if he knew the story, Dom Helder Camara writes, "So, in those most critical, most agonising of moments, we Christians have no right to forget that we are not born to die; we are born to live. We must hold on to hope, to inner peace, since we have the deep certainty of having been born for Easter, the everlasting Easter Day."[2]

Easter unfolds further good tidings for women who regret the futility of their work, an endless cycle of tasks repeated over and over. Although we laugh about the dinner that took an hour to prepare and an hour to clean up, that was wolfed down in ten minutes, a subtle bitterness lies beneath the surface amusement. Despite the highly publicized movement of women into the labor force, all studies agree that women who work outside the home still bear the bulk of the chores at home. However, Marie-Eloise Rosenblatt writes in "Women in the Passion and Resurrection Narratives," that in the passion narrative, women's work assumes a certain finality. When they approach the tomb with their spices, anointing the body is the last service they will do for someone they love.

But resurrection signifies a dramatic breakthrough: they will never perform these tasks again. "The new metaphor for women's work is no longer the cook pot or water jug."[3] The resurrection transforms their role into that of witnesses whose testimony is needed to convince the men. Their status has changed dramatically: from people who perform physical work related to biological needs to autonomous evangelizers who assert a spiritual experience. With their own inner lives reawakened, they become full participants in spreading the message of Jesus. As the chorus of praise rises on Easter, women who understand and appreciate their own transformed status can add an extra "Alleluia!"

FOR DISCUSSION AND REFLECTION

1. Remember receiving news or reaching insight so splendid it turned your world upside-down? Just as Joanna would never forget the words, "He is not here, but has risen," what words do you cherish years after they were spoken? In whose voice did you hear them? Here are some examples to prompt your own list:

   • "I'm so proud of you I can hardly speak."

   • "You passed the test (bar, board of licensing, or whatever . . .)."

   • "The first place award goes to_____" (fill in your name).

   • "I've been wanting for a long time to tell you how much I love you."

   • "The accident was serious, but your son or daughter survived."

   • "We can't find any more trace of your cancer."

   • "Your pregnancy test is positive/negative."

   • "I'm so lucky to have you."

   • "It looked impossible, but you did it!"

   Now add your own message of resurrection:

2. Joanna and her friends, while conscious of a major obstacle ahead ("Who will roll away the stone?") keep going.

    •   What does their stubborn persistence mean to you? Are they defying logic, or walking into another way of thinking?

    •   What stones block your path?

    •   When have you let these obstacles defeat you?

    •   When have you defeated the obstacles?

    If it is helpful, make a stone the focus for prayer. You may choose a formidable boulder, or an annoying "pebble in your shoe." The stone symbolizes the major or minor forces that seem impossible to get around: an infuriating or deadening relationship, a stalemate at work, a period of stagnancy in the creative life, an upcoming move or change, financial worries, a tough decision that cannot be postponed. As you reflect on the stone, consider how this question, raised by Michael Moynahan, S.J., has been asked or answered in your own life:

    > Who would have thought
    > the stones we stumbled over
    > would form the bridge
    > to all that lies beyond?[4]

3. One detail is strikingly similar in the stories of Joanna and the Samaritan woman (John 4:1–42). Both women carry a jar that is never used. Joanna never smells the embalming spices; the Samaritan woman abandons the water jar in her haste to spread the news of Jesus. Both women then become themselves the vessels for Jesus' story.

    In Jungian psychology, the container represents the boundaries of the self, providing our security. A journal can be such a container, as can a home, a job, or a family. Choose a vessel that represents your self at this moment.

Perhaps it's a homey soup bowl, a fragile crystal vase, a bottle of perfume, an earthenware coffee cup, a breadbasket. Turn it over in your hands or visualize it from every angle. Link it, if possible, to Joanna's jar. How is your best self contained there? Does the vessel leak or brim over? Does it nourish, give beauty or simply sit on the shelf right now? What do you like best about this vessel? Or, compare notes with a friend: what insights about each other do you gain from the symbol of the other person's container?

4. While we cherish the container and know that the bounded life is healthy, we must go a step further. We are also space for God, vessels of the divine. Sometimes we must risk expanding our self-imposed limitations in order to grow. In the popular phrase, "You were born to fly, but that cocoon has got to go."

    Karen Blixen (Isak Dinesen) played with this metaphor as she wrote a letter from Ngong, East Africa in 1926. The women of her day were criticized for their efforts to strike out on their own, because they could so easily get everything they wanted by riding on the back of a man, like a tiny goldcrest on the wings of an eagle. Blixen writes: "But what if we want to fly ourselves? What if we love wings and the air rushing past us?"[5]

    How have you answered this question in your own life? On three separate slips of paper, write down these three phrases:

    *   I will never . . .
    *   I cannot . . .
    *   I won't . . .

Complete each one. Then, as a symbol of your willingness to be surprised and enlarged by God, your eagerness to *fly*, tear up the cards.

5. While "remember" may not seem so central to Easter as words like "joy" or "life," it is crucial to Luke's account of the Resurrection. At the prompting of the angel, Joanna and her friends remember the words of Jesus, and their memory becomes the basis for telling the community that Jesus is alive. Marie-Eloise Rosenblatt writes: "Women's memory is evidently the touchstone for the community's faith."[6]

How is that still true in your experience? How do the memories of grandmothers or other foremothers sustain the faith today? Reach into your own memory; center on one woman who has served as such a pillar. What serves to kindle the memory of her? (While Luke attributes remembering to the angel's prompting, various other sources might stir the memory today: a story or scent, a taste or a fragment of music, a poem . . .) What blessing does the memory of this woman bring?

19

Mrs. Cleopas:
Seven-Mile Trudge, Seven-Mile Flight

(LUKE 24:13–35)

The road to Emmaus stretched long and dry as my husband and I set out that day. Both Cleopas and I were depressed.

"Why can't we stay another day?" I'd protested to him as we packed.

"We've been gone too long already. Time to get home." Cleopas wouldn't change his mind.

"But these rumors—I want to find out. Salome and Joanna say . . . "

"They're hysterical. Don't get involved. Besides, we're all exhausted."

"Well, tired and depressed isn't the greatest way to start a journey!"

At least I'd voiced my objections, I thought as we trudged towards Emmaus. But I can read my husband. Under the anger hides a sadness. Not knowing what to do with that terrible image of crucifixion in his mind, unable to reconcile the criminal's death with his knowledge of Jesus, he balks like a mule. I tried to draw him into conversation.

"You know, I really like our friends in Jerusalem. Mary says the same thing I do: around Jesus, we were *somebody*. Free. Alive."

Cleopas hadn't quite absorbed Jesus' attitude.

"He was probably just another fake. And we were wrong to believe him. Let's try to forget it."

"But I'll never forget him," I said. "His stories. His laughter. His touch."

Cleopas seemed determined to erase those memories. "I hope he never touched *you*. And forget that freedom talk or the Romans will jail you, too."

But he had touched me, in a way I couldn't explain to Cleopas. Around him, I felt stronger, more confident—yet at the same time, more compassionate. It was a relief when a stranger joined us. Maybe he could distract us from this impasse.

Something pulled at me as he talked, like my son, insistent at my sleeve. I grew more excited, more hopeful than I've felt since Jesus died. Almost as if . . .

Anyway, when I invited him to stay and he accepted, I was thrilled. How crazy: We'd been away, no food in the house, a guest for dinner, and I was *pleased*? Quickly, I borrowed food from my neighbor.

When the stranger reached for the pita bread, I almost warned him it might be stale. But something about his cupped hands prompted a memory and awakened a yearning that hadn't died after all. Where had I seen that gesture before?

Mrs. Cleopas Today

Jesus' disclosure of himself to those who are "on the road" comes as good news to people who are often in motion. While some may criticize the frenzied mobility of our era, Jesus joins the journey. In *Generous Lives: American Catholic Women Today*, Jane Redmont writes, "commuting time seems to have become the privileged place of prayer in North America."[1] Along similar lines, Thomas Moore says in *Soul Mates*, "Walking can be a soul activity, so long as it is not done for some heroic purpose such as getting somewhere, losing weight, or winning a race."[2] Thus, Cleopas and his unnamed companion (had he been male, he would have been named) in Luke 24:13–35 seem like contemporaries, on the move.

There are also striking parallels between Jesus' actions and contemporary thought on how to help people overwhelmed by a tragedy. In *Images of Hope*, William Lynch writes a description that could fit the Emmaus dynamic: "The imagination is "the gift that constantly proposes to itself that the boundaries of the possible are wider than they seem."[3] This ability enables us to escape entrapment in various "prisons of the impossible," and to avoid mistaking a part for the whole. He cites the example of Harry Stack Sullivan, who would ask his patients to recall at what precise time a traumatic incident had occurred. Placing the event in the larger context of time makes it less absolute and frees the imagination to fight its way out of the dreary cage of the instant.[4] When Jesus invites the couple bound for Emmaus to talk about the events that have transpired in the last three days, he places the Crucifixion in the context of time and space.

Freud's basic principle for restoring mental health was that whatever came to mind in doctor–patient relationships should be discussed. The severely depressed person, who distrusts words would reply, "What's the use?" and remain hopelessly paralyzed. So Luke's Gospel records that the two companions stopped short, immobilized by sorrow. When Jesus invites the disciples to talk about the Crucifixion, they resume their walk. Furthermore, they journey into recognition and elation.

It is especially appealing to note that they recognized him, not in formal worship or in a church setting, but at the kitchen table, in the simplest gesture of breaking bread. The Christian church began in the home, growing from a long

Jewish tradition of domestic prayer and ritual. As Jesus' presence there affirms, the household is holy ground.

Many people, alienated from formal worship in large, impersonal churches are recovering the depth of celebration at home: with family, small Christian communities, or women's prayer groups. The Emmaus revelation showed not only something about Jesus, but also something about us: that our most ordinary routines can be sacramental, that we can move beyond despair, that our times and spaces are sacred.

For Discussion and Reflection

1. The story ends on a question mark. On your own, continue Mrs. Cleopas' thoughts.

2. William Barry says it is important to remember and relate our "touchstone" experiences of God so we can recognize God again in a new situation. What was the touchstone experience for Mrs. Cleopas?

   Now, mentally place yourself in the setting where you are happiest. Relish the detail: Walking through fresh snow, encircled by the arms of a beloved person, eating a meal with those you love, working at a challenging project, climbing a mountain. How do you experience God there?

   Or try another version, asking yourself or a partner: What are my most powerful experiences of God? (Remember they can be as homely as stale bread.) Draw, write about, or discuss the hints (such as those that coalesce around the breaking of bread) that help you recognize the presence of Christ.

3. Remember special times when you have broken bread or shared wine with friends. What is holy in those memories? Why do you think Jesus chose the meal to unveil his identity, preferring this setting to many other possibilities?

4. Imagine a loved one who has died. In what ways does he or she return to you and make that beloved presence felt?

5. What connection do you find between the long walk or the long drive and the coming to insight? Name the journeys in your life (either daily ones or rare ones) in which ordinary terrain has turned to prayerful place.

    Contrast these with the frustrations of being caught in a traffic jam, stalled with a dead battery, or stranded at an airport in a blizzard. How does being immobilized help you understand the hopelessness Mr. and Mrs. Cleopas felt before Christ joined them along the road? Has anyone ever extended to you the kind of help Jesus gives, to get them moving again? Linger for a while with that memory . . .

6. If you participate in a group or enjoy bodily prayer, you may want to close this book with ritual. Through motion or gesture, show how Mrs. Cleopas trudged to Emmaus, and how she returned to Jerusalem.

7. Now that you have met these hidden women of the Gospels, in what ways has your viewpoint shifted? Knowing that they are not too different from women today, what steps in a new direction will you now take? How will you continue to journey with them, inviting them into your future?

MATRILINEAGE

Before the cross slit
the sky of Chartres,
before the stone sign
anchored Celtic graves
or a thumb with oil
printed a Roman forehead,

Blandita the slave girl
hung on a post, morsel
for wild animals and
sport to entertain Lyon.
As fangs gnawed bone,
she hung in form of cross.

Her agony stirred memory
and other martyrs read
in her his ransom: again
torn flesh, convulsion,
scandal, the bleary eyes
as love keeps watch.

And still we read you,
Maura, Ita, Dorothy, Jean,
Elba and Celina Ramos,
sisters in Liberia: your
limbs stretched to impossible
contours of crucifix.

Endnotes

INTRODUCTION

1. Sherry Anderson and Patricia Hopkins, *The Feminine Face of God* (New York: Bantam Books, 1992), 49.
2. Carolyn Osiek, *Beyond Anger: On Being a Feminist in the Church* (New York: Paulist Press, 1986), 34.
3. Elizabeth Johnson, *She Who Is: The Mystery of God in Feminist Theological Discourse* (New York: Crossroad, 1993), 38.
4. Carol Newsom and Sharon Ringe, eds., *The Women's Bible Commentary* (Louisville, Ky.: Westminster/John Knox Press, 1992), 282.

CHAPTER I

1. Osiek, 34.
2. Sofia Cavalletti, *The Religious Potential of the Child* (New York: Paulist Press, 1983), 71.
3. S. Marie Schwan and Jacqueline Bergen, *Freedom: A Guide for Prayer* (Winona, Minn.: St. Mary's Press, 1988), 73.

CHAPTER 2

1. Nathan Mitchell, *Eucharist as Sacrament of Initiation* (Chicago: Liturgy Training Publications, 1994), 6.
2. Clarissa Pinkola Estes, *Women Who Run With the Wolves* (New York: Ballantine Books, 1992), 222.
3. Toni Morrison, quoted in Julia Cameron, *The Artist's Way* (New York: Putnam's, 1992), 97.
4. Mary Daly, quoted in Cameron, 2.
5. Gloria Naylor, *Mama Day* (New York: Ticknor & Fields, 1988), 59.
6. Estes, 408.

CHAPTER 3

1. Anne Morrow Lindbergh, "Second Sowing," *Hour of Gold, Hour of Lead* (New York: Signet, 1973), 183.
2. Quoted in Sara Ruddick. *Maternal Thinking: Toward a Politics of Peace* (New York: Ballantine Books, 1989), 231.
3. Patricia Donovan, quoted in Rosemary Radford Ruether, *Women-Church: Theology and Practice of Feminist Liturgical Communities* (San Francisco: Harper & Row, 1985), 233.
4. Dorothee Soëlle, *Stations of the Cross: A Latin American Pilgrimage* (Minneapolis: Fortress Press, 1993), 43.

CHAPTER 4

1. Mary Belenky and others, *Women's Ways of Knowing* (New York: Basic Books, 1986), 199.
2. Louise Bogan, quoted in Cameron, 33.

CHAPTER 5

1. Wendy Wright, *Sacred Dwelling* (Leavenworth, Kan.: Forest of Peace Publishing, 1994), 32–33.
2. Anderson and Hopkins, 45–71.
3. Wright, 139.
4. Virginia Woolf, "What if Shakespeare Had Had a Sister?" from *A Room of One's Own,* in Richard Abcarian and Marvin Klotz, eds., *Literature: The Human Experience* (New York: St. Martin's Press, 1988), 361–68.
5. Thomas Merton, quoted in Esther de Waal, *A Seven Day Journey with Thomas Merton* (Ann Arbor, Mich.: Servant Publications, 1992), 77.
6. Estes, 29, 31.
7. William Barry, *Allowing the Creator to Deal with the Creature* (New York: Paulist Press, 1994), 39.
8. Peig Sayers, quoted in Robert Wicks, *Touching the Holy* (Notre Dame, Ind.: Ave Maria Press, 1993), 145.
9. John Macmurray, *Persons in Relation* (London: Faber & Faber, 1961), 171.
10. Etty Hillesum, *An Interrupted Life* (New York: Washington Square Press/Pocket Books, 1985), 187.

CHAPTER 7

1. Mary Catherine Bateson, *Composing a Life* (New York: Penguin Books, 1990), 166.
2. Macrina Wiederkehr, *A Tree Full of Angels* (San Francisco: HarperCollins, 1988), 153.
3. James Dunning, *Echoing God's Word* (Arlington, Va.: North American Forum on the Catechumenate, 1993), 278.

CHAPTER 8

1. Dom Helder Camara, *The Gospel with Dom Helder Camara*, trans. Alan Neame (London: Daron, Longman & Todd, 1986), 74.

CHAPTER 9

1. Megan McKenna, *Not Counting Women and Children* (Maryknoll, N.Y.: Orbis Books, 1994), 154–59.
2. Alice Walker, *Possessing the Secret of Joy* (New York: Harcourt Brace, 1992), 281.
3. Dottie Lamm, "What World Will We Leave Our Daughters?" *Denver Post* (September 3, 1995), D4.
4. Madonna Kolbenschlag, ed., *Women in the Church I* (Washington, D.C.: The Pastoral Press, 1987), 206–7
5. Maya Angelou, "Our Grandmothers," *The Complete Collected Poems of Maya Angelou* (New York: Random House, 1994), 254.
6. Miriam Therese Winter, Adair Lummis, and Allison Stokes, *Defecting in Place: Women Claiming Responsibility for Their Own Spiritual Lives* (New York: Crossroad, 1994), 38.
7. Ibid., 43.
8. Kolbenschlag, 210.
9. McKenna, 156.
10. Toni Cade Bambara, quoted in Sharon Welch, *A Feminist Ethic of Risk* (Minneapolis: Augsburg Fortress, 1990), 18.
11. Julie Olsen Edwards, quoted in Ruddick, 81.
12. McKenna, 160.

CHAPTER 10

1. Newsom and Ringe, 282.
2. Thomas Moore, *Care of the Soul* (New York: HarperCollins, 1992), 27.

CHAPTER 11

1. Winter et al., 94.
2. David Brower. "Fighting for the Earth." *The Denver Post Magazine* (April 2, 1995), 11.
3. Edna St. Vincent Millay, "Dirge Without Music," in Louis Untermeyer, ed., *A Concise Treasury of Great Poems* (New York: Pocket Books, 1962), 495.
4. Marshall Sprague, *Sometimes I'm Happy: A Writer's Memoir* (Athens, Ohio: Swallow Press/ Ohio University Press, 1995), 152.
5. *National Catholic Reporter* (January 20, 1995), 25.

CHAPTER 12

1. Isak Dinesen, "Letter to Mary Bess Westenholz," *Letters from Africa: 1914–1931*. Ed. Frans Lasson, (Chicago: University of Chicago Press, 1981), 260.
2. T. S. Eliot, "Four Quartets," *Collected Poems, 1909–1962* (New York: Harcourt, Brace & World, 1963), 189.
3. Bateson, 3–4, 9.
4. Dorothy Day, quoted in "Words for Quiet Moments." *Catholic Digest* (August 1995), 89.
5. Mechthild of Magdeburg, quoted in Carol Flinders, *Enduring Grace* (San Francisco: Harper, 1993), 52.
6. Abraham Joshua Heschel, quoted in "Words for Quiet Moments," 90.
7. Edwina Gateley, quoted in "Burdens and Breakthroughs: An Interview with Edwina Gateley," by Don Beaulieu, *The Other Side* (May/June, 1995), 10.
8. Richard Rohr, *Radical Grace* (Cincinnati, Ohio: St. Anthony Messenger Press, 1995), 320–21.

CHAPTER 13

1. Dunning, 241.
2. Belenky et al., 84.

3. Deborah Tannen, *You Just Don't Understand! Women and Men in Conversation* (New York: William Morrow, 1990), 25.
4. Belenky et al., 189.
5. Millay, "Dirge Without Music," 495.
6. Zora Neale Hurston, *Their Eyes Were Watching God*, in *Novels and Stories* (New York: Penguin Books, Literary Classics of the United States, 1995), 279.
7. Newsom and Ringe, eds., 299.
8. Mary Oliver, "In Blackwater Woods." *White Pine* (New York: Harcourt Brace, 1994), 32.

CHAPTER 14

1. William Barry, *Finding God in All Things* (Notre Dame, Ind.: Ave Maria Press, 1991), 66–75.
2. Mitchell, 95.
3. Marcus Borg, *Meeting Jesus Again for the First Time* (San Francisco: HarperCollins, 1994), 57.
4. Esther de Waal, *Every Earthly Blessing* (Ann Arbor, MI: Servant Publications, 1991), 25.
5. Ibid.
6. Bateson, 128.

CHAPTER 15

1. Belenky et al., 167.
2. Ibid., 68.
3. Teresa of Avila, quoted in Flinders, 185.
4. Winter et al., 38.
5. Ibid., 81.
6. Ibid., 46–47.
7. Ariel Miller, "The Philadelphia 11." *The Witness* (July, 1994), 14.
8. Carter Heyward, quoted in Miller, 15.
9. Mary Daly, *Beyond God the Father* (Boston: Beacon Press, 1973), 19.
10. Winter et al., 97.
11. Joseph Tetlow, *Ignatius Loyola: Spiritual Exercises* (New York: Crossroad, 1992), 53.
12. William Lynch, *Images of Hope* (Baltimore: Helicon Press, 1965), 175.

13. Gerald O'Collins, "An Easter Healing of Memories," *America* 166:13, 322–23.

14. John Bookser Feister, "Rebuild My Church: An Interview with Richard Rohr, O.F.M.," *St. Anthony Messenger* (July 1995), 16.

CHAPTER 16

1. Newsom and Ringe, eds., 279.

CHAPTER 17

1. Marie-Eloise Rosenblatt, "Women in the Passion and Resurrection Narratives," *The Way* Supplement 74 (Summer 1992), 45.

2. Jessica Powers, "One Answer," quoted in Marcianne Kappes. *Track of the Mystic: The Spirituality of Jessica Powers* (Kansas City: Sheed & Ward, 1994), 112.

3. Dunning, 241.

4. Julian of Norwich, quoted in Rosenblatt, 43.

CHAPTER 18

1. Jon Sobrino, S.J., quoted in Johnson, 74.

2. Helder Camara, 76.

3. Rosenblatt, 46.

4. Michael Moynahan, *Orphaned Wisdom: Meditations for Lent* (New York: Paulist Press, 1990), 99.

5. Dinesen, 262.

6. Rosenblatt, 49.

CHAPTER 19

1. Jane Redmont, *Generous Lives: American Catholic Women Today* (New York: Morrow, 1992), 96.

2. Thomas Moore, *Soul Mates* (New York: HarperCollins, 1994), 117.

3. Lynch, 35.

4. Ibid., 254.

Bibliography

Anderson, Sherry and Patricia Hopkins. *The Feminine Face of God*. New York: Bantam Books, 1992.

Angelou, Maya. "Our Grandmothers," *The Complete Collected Poems of Maya Angelou*. New York: Random House, 1994.

Barry, William, *Allowing the Creator to Deal with the Creature*. New York: Paulist Press, 1994.

———. *Finding God in All Things*. Notre Dame, Ind.: Ave Maria Press, 1991.

Bateson, Mary Catherine. *Composing a Life*. New York: Penguin Books, 1990.

Belenky, Mary and others. *Women's Ways of Knowing*. New York: Basic Books, 1986.

Bookser Feister, John. "Rebuild My Church: An Interview with Richard Rohr, O.F.M.," *St. Anthony Messenger* (July 1995).

Borg, Marcus. *Meeting Jesus Again for the First Time*. San Francisco: HarperCollins, 1994.

Brower, David. "Fighting for the Earth." *The Denver Post Magazine* (April 2, 1995), 11.

Camara, Dom Helder. *The Gospel with Dom Helder Camara*, trans. Alan Neame. London: Daron, Longman & Todd, 1986.

Cameron, Julia. *The Artist's Way*. New York: Putnam's, 1992.

Cavalletti, Sofia. *The Religious Potential of the Child*. New York: Paulist Press, 1983.

Daly, Mary. *Beyond God the Father*. Boston: Beacon Press, 1973.

de Waal, Esther. *A Seven Day Journey with Thomas Merton.* Ann Arbor, Mich.: Servant Publications, 1992.

———. *Every Earthly Blessing.* Ann Arbor, Mich.: Servant Publications, 1991.

Dinesen, Isak. "Letter to Mary Bess Westenholz," *Letters from Africa: 1914–1931.* Ed. Frans Lasson. Chicago: University of Chicago Press, 1981.

Dunning, James. *Echoing God's Word.* Arlington, Va.: North American Forum on the Catechumenate, 1993.

Eliot, T. S. "Four Quartets," *Collected Poems, 1909–1962.* New York: Harcourt, Brace & World, 1963.

Estes, Clarissa Pinkola. *Women Who Run With the Wolves.* New York: Ballantine Books, 1992.

Flinders, Carol. *Enduring Grace.* San Francisco: HarperSanFrancisco, 1993.

Gateley, Edwina. quoted in "Burdens and Breakthroughs: An Interview with Edwina Gateley," by Don Beaulieu, *The Other Side* (May/June, 1995), 10.

Hillesum, Etty. *An Interrupted Life.* New York: Washington Square Press, Pocket Books, 1985.

Hurston, Zora Neale. *Their Eyes Were Watching God* in *Novels and Stories.* New York: Penguin Books, Literary Classics of the United States, 1995.

Johnson, Elizabeth. *She Who Is: The Mystery of God in Feminist Theological Discourse.* New York: Crossroad, 1993.

Kolbenschlag, Madonna. ed.. *Women in the Church I.* Washington, D.C.: The Pastoral Press, 1987.

Lamm, Dottie. "What World Will We Leave Our Daughters?" *Denver Post* (September 3, 1995), D4.

Lindbergh, Anne Morrow. "Second Sowing," *Hour of Gold, Hour of Lead.* New York: Signet, 1973.

Lynch, William. *Images of Hope.* Baltimore, Md.: Helicon Press, 1965.

Macmurray, John. *Persons in Relation.* London: Faber & Faber, 1961.

McKenna, Megan. *Not Counting Women and Children.* Maryknoll, NY: Orbis Books, 1994.

Miller, Ariel. "The Philadelphia 11." *The Witness* (July, 1994).

Mitchell, Nathan. *Eucharist as Sacrament of Initiation.* Chicago: Liturgy Training Publications, 1994.

Moore, Thomas. *Care of the Soul.* New York: HarperCollins Publishers, 1992.

_____. *Soul Mates.* New York: HarperCollins Publishers, 1994.

Moynahan, Michael. *Orphaned Wisdom: Meditations for Lent.* New York: Paulist Press, 1990.

Naylor, Gloria. *Mama Day.* New York: Ticknor & Fields, 1988.

Newsom, Carol and Sharon Ringe, eds. *The Women's Bible Commentary.* Louisville, Ky.: Westminster/John Knox Press, 1992.

O'Collins, Gerald. "An Easter Healing of Memories," *America* 166:13, 322–23.

Oliver, Mary. "In Blackwater Woods." *White Pine.* New York: Harcourt Brace Jovanovich, 1994.

Osiek, Carolyn. *Beyond Anger: On Being a Feminist in the Church.* New York: Paulist Press, 1986.

Powers, Jessica. "One Answer," quoted in Marcianne Kappes. *Track of the Mystic: The Spirituality of Jessica Powers.* Kansas City: Sheed & Ward, 1994.

Redmont, Jane. *Generous Lives: American Catholic Women Today.* New York: Morrow, 1992.

Ruether, Rosemary Radford. *Women-Church: Theology and Practice of Feminist Liturgical Communities*. San Francisco: Harper & Row, 1985.

Rohr, Richard. *Radical Grace*. Cincinnati, Ohio: St. Anthony Messenger Press, 1995.

Rosenblatt, Marie-Eloise. "Women in the Passion and Resurrection Narratives," *The Way* Supplement 74 (Summer 1992).

Ruddick, Sara. *Maternal Thinking: Toward a Politics of Peace*. New York: Ballantine Books, 1989.

Schwan, S. Marie and Jacqueline Bergen. *Freedom: A Guide for Prayer*. Winona, Minn.: St. Mary's Press, 1988.

Soëlle, Dorothee. *Stations of the Cross: A Latin American Pilgrimage*. Minneapolis: Fortress Press, 1993.

Sprague, Marshall. *Sometimes I'm Happy: A Writer's Memoir*. Athens, Ohio: Swallow Press/ Ohio University Press, 1995.

St. Vincent Millay, Edna. "Dirge Without Music." in Louis Untermeyer, Ed. *A Concise Treasury of Great Poems*. New York: Pocket Books, 1962.

Tannen, Deborah. *You Just Don't Understand! Women and Men in Conversation*. New York: William Morrow, 1990.

Tetlow, Joseph. *Ignatius Loyola: Spiritual Exercises*. New York: Crossroad, 1992.

Walker, Alice. *Possessing the Secret of Joy*. New York: Harcourt Brace, 1992.

Welch, Sharon. *A Feminist Ethic of Risk*. Minneapolis: Augsburg Fortress, 1990.

Wicks, Robert. *Touching the Holy*. Notre Dame, Ind.: Ave Maria Press, 1993.

Wiederkehr, Macrina. *A Tree Full of Angels*. San Francisco: HarperCollins, 1988.

Winter, Miriam Therese, Adair Lummis and Allison Stokes, *Defecting in Place: Women Claiming Responsibility for Their Own Spiritual Lives*. New York: Crossroad, 1994.

Winter, Miriam Therese. *The Gospel According To Mary*. New York: Crossroad, 1993.

Woolf, Virginia. "What if Shakespeare Had Had a Sister?" from *A Room of One's Own* in Richard Abcarian and Marvin Klotz,eds. *Literature: the Human Experience*. New York: St. Martin's Press, 1988, 361–68.

Wright, Wendy. *Sacred Dwelling*. Leavenworth, Kan.: Forest of Peace Publishing, 1994.

Acknowledgments

The following selections written by Kathy Coffey appeared originally in the publications listed below:

"Annunciation" in *St. Anthony Messenger* and Abbey Press *Prayer Notes*

"The Other Grandmother" in *Theology Today*

"Mary Reads the Gospel" in *St. Anthony Messenger*

"Lilith and Jacob Reminisce," originally entitled "The Cana Couple Reminisce," in *St. Anthony Messenger* and *Marriage Encounter Magazine*

"Feeding Five Thousand—and Me," in *St. Anthony Messenger*

"Wife of Jairus," in *St. Anthony Messenger*

"The First Ressurection Appearance," in *St. Anthony Messenger* and *Theology Today*

"Matrilineage" in *St. Anthony Messenger* and *Theology Today*

Parts of "Bread and Cup for Each Other: Women Meditate on Eucharist" appeared in *St. Anthony Messenger* under the title "A Mother's Perspective on the Eucharist"

Of Related Interest

Soul Sisters
Women in Scripture Speak to Women Today
Edwina Gateley
Art by Louis Glanzman
144 pages, 12 full-color illustrations
ISBN 1-57075-443-8 Paperback

"In painting and in poetry this book contemplates the women who knew Jesus: our soul sisters if we look deeply enough."
—*Sister Wendy Beckett*

"When I first saw Louis Glanzman's paintings of twelve women in the gospels whose names are so familiar, something happened inside me. It was as if I suddenly recognized beloved sisters whom I had never seen before but knew in my heart.
These paintings, with their subtle colors and expressive faces, had a life of their own—unique, powerful, and as real as any living woman. The faces rose from the prints and spoke to me. After a lifetime of knowing all about these women I felt, at last, that I had actually met them."
—*Edwina Gateley*

Please support your local bookstore, or call 1-800-258-5838.
For a free catalogue, please write us at
Orbis Books, Box 308
Maryknoll NY 10545-0308
Or visit our website and order online at
www.orbisbooks.org

Thank you for reading *Hidden Women of the Gospels*.
We hope you enjoyed it.

Women & Christianity
Volume I: The First Thousand Years
Mary T. Malone
ISBN 1-57075-365-2 Hardcover
ISBN 1-57075-366-0 Paperback

"This excellent book is the first volume in what promises to be an invaluable series on the history of women in the Christian tridition. It is a welcome addition to the literature, well grounded, accessible, and able to inform even as it raises consciousness."
—*Mary Jo Weaver, Indiana University*

Women & Christianity
Volume II: From 1000 to the Reformation
Mary T. Malone
ISBN 1-57075-394-6 Hardcover
ISBN 1-57075-393-8 Paperback

The second volume in a major historical trilogy that documents the lives and contributions of Christian women from the beginning of Christianity to the present.

To be published in Fall, 2003
Women & Christianity
Volume III: From the Reformation to the 21st Century
Mary T. Malone
ISBN 1-57075-476-4 Hardcover
ISBN 1-57075-475-6 Paperback

The final volume in a major historical trilogy that documents the lives and contributions of Christian women from the beginnings of Christianity to the present.